CHRISTMAS: MYTH, MAGIC *and* LEGEND

Making sense of the Christmas stories

JOHN QUERIPEL

WIPF & STOCK · Eugene, Oregon

Wipf and Stock Publishers
199 W 8th Ave, Suite 3
Eugene, OR 97401

Christmas: Myth, Magic and Legend
Making sense of the Christmas stories
By Queripel, John
Copyright © 2018 by Queripel, John All rights reserved.
Softcover ISBN-13: 979-8-3852-4168-2
Hardcover ISBN-13: 979-8-3852-4169-9
eBook ISBN-13: 979-8-3852-4170-5
Publication date 12/18/2024
Previously published by Morning Star Publishing, 2018

This edition is a scanned facsimile of the original edition published in 2018.

Contents

Preface 5

1: A myth is not a lie. 9

2: 'The' Christmas Story? 25

3: The Family Tree 39

4: Virgin Mother!. 53

5: Meet the family 75

6: O little town of Nazareth. 87

7: Massacre at Bethlehem 107

8: The Heavenly portents tell? 115

9: Who is the greatest? 125

10: Why the stories? 135

Preface

One of the greatest memories we carry through our lives is of how when we were young the world was infused with magic, Santa Claus, the Easter Bunny, fairies in the bottom of the garden and much more magic which filled our lives. We would wake to Christmas Day surrounded by the gifts which Santa Claus had mysteriously and secretly placed there. I even remember setting a trap to catch 'Santa' in the act of distributing my gifts. I can only assume my parents were sufficiently nimble of foot to not trip up. As we grew we wondered just how it was possible for Santa to do that, not just for us but for children right around the world with such incredible speed. Some of us even began to ponder why it was that Santa was not so generous to children in poorer countries or even to poorer children we may have known. Our critical thinking was kicking in before finally taking us to the point where no longer could we hold Santa Claus to be real though I suppose few of us can remember the specific point where our belief in Santa died. That we mostly fail to do so tells me that the process was not overwhelming or devastating. Our lives went on and indeed we continued to celebrate Christmas, perhaps in a religious manner or one totally secular in style.

Though in our lives the magic gradually died, we still as adults yearn for it. How we enjoy, especially at Christmas, playing the magical games of our children and grand-children, participating in their magical view of the world, though always knowing of course that such magic doesn't really exist.

In this work, I want to argue that Christmas has become a magical game we enjoy playing, a game that takes us back to our childhood magic, one in which we are prepared to put aside our adulthood with all its critical faculties. Indeed, I believe, so powerful has this motivation become it has served to strip away from Christmas nearly all its real meaning. In saying this I don't mean primarily for those who have rejected the religious meaning of Christmas, settling for a secular or even a hedonistic view, but rather am referring particularly to those still either intensely or loosely holding to religious interpretations. So sentimental has the story become and so comfortable are we with all the magic, images and symbols that even as people of faith we have often lost sight of the true significance and importance of what is being signified by Christmas. The symbols have largely precluded us from really seeing what is being symbolised! I intend to strip away the magic and the myth believing that, as was in the case of our loss of faith in Santa Claus, fairies at the bottom of the garden, or the Easter Bunny, the process will not be one which will destroy us. Indeed, I believe, it will be one which both confirms and enriches us in understanding just what the Christmas story really signifies.

There will be some who will be upset, perhaps even offended by the title of this book, 'Christmas: Myth, Magic and Legend.' That will probably be because they fail to understand the power of all that is represented in those three words, too simply equating my saying that the nativity stories are such with meaning that they have no truth in them. That is of course to conflate truth with factual truth and to neglect other forms of truth. It is to fail to understand particularly the depth of what is meant by the term myth but also not to appreciate the power of magic, especially as we have already seen when it comes to the Christmas story, while finally, it doesn't appreciate how legends attach themselves to any story. In response to this challenge I have posed, to move beyond the literalisms of the Christmas story, many will choose one of two options. Some will rigorously hold to a literal understanding of the story believing the events therein described, no matter how different they are to the norm, as being real events, which passed in the flow of history. Others will simply 'throw out the baby with the bathwater' stating that if the Christmas stories are not true literally they will argue then there is simply no truth in the story per-se. Both responses are wrong in that they essentially represent two sides of the same coin marked literalism. If a truth is not literal it will be argued by both these groups, then it need be false. Truth I wish to suggest is far more multi-faceted than that.

The Christmas stories, and perhaps some will be surprised that I use the plural as the two stories have become so conflated in our minds, are neither factually true but nor are they false. Rather they are creative constructions by the writers, Matthew and Luke [1] to communicate what they each held as very deep truths, those which moved deeply beyond the realm of the literal or factual into the areas which I have identified, myth, magic and legend. When we speak of these things as alternative forms of truth I am reminded of the story about the North Amerindian leader Black Hawk who after completing a story added, 'I am not sure if it actually happened this way, but I know the story is true.' Like many stories the Christmas stories may not have literally happened the way in which they are told but still contained within each there is profound truth. To find that we need first, as we inevitably do at Christmas, take off the wrapping, as attractive and appealing as that wrapping may be, so to find the real gift contained inside.

Before doing that, we need however first understand the wrapping, that wrapping of course being the story itself, couched in myth, magic and legend. There is magic as I suggested in the Christmas narrative and we find the magic of flying reindeer and an obese Santa, despite his girth, being able to move at tremendous speed and fit down tight chimneys to complete his worldwide gift round overnight, highly attractive. Further there is the deeper magic of the stories as a whole. Magic is about transformation or transmogrification and it is at this level that the deepest magic of the Christmas stories attaches in that we are transformed by them being taken by them into another world. Legends also get attached to the story, especially after the biblical period with figures like St Nicolas from whom we get Santa Claus, through such stories as St Wenceslas right up to the entry of Rudolf and the fellow reindeers in recent times, but is with the deeper question of myth with which we will be spending most time.

Far from upsetting us, this necessity of seeking an alternative deeper truth and meaning should be welcomed as a process whereby in speaking of and celebrating Christmas we no longer need to lay aside our critical thinking, the very critical thinking which makes us adults. As adults then we will be able to better grasp the true and depth meaning of Christmas and again be challenged by what it says to us. This is the journey on which I wish to take us in this work.

It is to understanding myth to which we must now turn.

Endnotes

1 Scholars have long known that the gospels were not written by the person whose name is ascribed to them. Rather they are the final product of a creative process which occurred within the early Christian communities. A final editor or redactor then completed the process and, as was a common habit in the ancient world feeling they were not worthy to have their name associated with the gospel, chose a more significant figure, usually in this case, one of the apostles, in the early church with which to associate the gospel. For convenience, I will use of course the names ascribed to the gospels.

1: A MYTH IS NOT A LIE

What is the meaning of Christmas? In Christian terms, it speaks of the incarnation (literally the entering flesh) of God in Jesus Christ. The Christmas stories are attempts at showing how this happened and their means of doing this is to build both on older pagan stories, which long preceded these stories, while also making use of stories from the Hebrew Scriptures, what Christians call the Old Testament. [1] By use of these older stories and myths the gospel writers seek to make sense of their claim that Jesus was divine, God incarnate and was so, according to the Christmas stories, from the time of his birth. It is this theological concern which necessitates the stories and utterly shapes them. As such the stories, the gospel writers give us, are never intended to be taken as factual truths but rather as means using myth to assert the gospel writers, (and here we are speaking of only two of the, Matthew and Luke) beliefs concerning Jesus' divinity. Shaped by myth the stories represent expressions of those beliefs.

It pursuing the meaning of the Christmas stories it is crucially important we understand just what myth is. To the modern ear myth, as said, usually equates to untruth. That however is to do a great injustice to the depth of what is represented by this word. All world cultures create stories which speak profound truths to them in order to make sense of the world around them and give explication to their situation. Traditionally there has been no need within these societies to raise the question as to whether these stories were literally or factually true. Indeed, for most peoples, as we have seen with Black Hawk, this sort of question would have been inconceivable and nonsensical if put to them, for the equation of fact and truth is a modern equation.

Much of the difficulty, particularly for those of us in the West have in understanding myth comes from our living in a modern scientific world. [2] This outlook tends to lead us to equate truth with that which is factual or can be measure. As products of the modern Western scientific mindset this is our training and it is deeply ingrained in us even if our scientific knowledge is only rudimentary. Science, as commonly understood, is an inductive process of experimentation and observation, along with an understanding that repeating the same experiment will give the same result assuming a dispassionate experimenter not allowing any bias or commitment to the experiment being conducted to influence the results while they hold constant all other variables to that being examined. Repetition of the experiment giving the same result allows the experimenter to make a claim, that they have proved a thing true with all other conjectures being shown to be wrong. Science thus understood, sees truth as facts being objectively verifiable or not. Thus, let us assume a scientist wants to investigate the boiling point of water. They will carry out an experiment of heating water and then note the temperature where it changes from liquid form to gaseous form. Of course, we know they will find that the temperature at which this occurs is 100 degrees Celsius. That scientist having carried out the experiment numerous times will conclude that water always boils at 100 degrees C so that they, having proved the fact by experiment can make a scientific claim regarding the boiling point of water. However, one day another scientist who enjoys mountaineering will stop and boil their billy for a cup of tea while at Base Camp on Mount Everest. That scientist however finds that the tea he normally so enjoys is not so enjoyable this time with tea leaves still floating on the top. This shouldn't be the case surely, he or she will conclude as the water was clearly observed boiling. After carrying out numerous repeated experiments they will find of course that the scientific maxim that water boils at 100 degrees C is only true at sea-level. An unpredicted variable had entered the original experiment with the change of altitude. A tightening of the scientific conclusion is needed then to say that at sea level water boils at 100 degrees C. This is how science is normally understood; rigorous testing continually tightening scientific statements. Clearly in this simple example of science we note something can't be false and, yet the conclusion remain valid for science operates by something being proved true, and thus being proved true makes other conjectures false. Truth and falsehood are necessarily opposed. Indeed, just a single factual evidence of water boiling at a temperature not 100 degrees C, as we have just seen, means the universal statement that water always boils at that temperature is no

1: A myth is not a lie

longer true. The statement must then be restated, as above, until perhaps another single case observation again proves the new premise not true. Truth and falsity are understood as opposites, both absolute, so that just one single falsity destroys a truth.

This builds on the logical maxims spoken by Aristotle some 2,500 years ago by which a statement can't be both true and false, and that there is also an excluded middle in that something can't be half true and half false. This Aristotelian logic has profoundly shaped our understanding so that we have come to believe that truth must be factual, objective and verifiable and that which is not true in such manner necessarily is false.

Myth however as we have seen, clearly doesn't fit anywhere within this definition of truth. It should be noted in passing that science itself is not synonymous with the above popular understanding with the field of quantum physics making it very clear that 'scientific truth' is not so easily found. In quantum physics the idea of the objective vantage point of the observer or experimenter having no effect on the observation no longer holds for what we seek to explore will determine what we will find i.e. there is no subject objectivity, while also the Heisenberg uncertainty principle comes into play meaning that further results are not predictable in the way we would like them to be but are rather only probabilities. Science is a far different and more complicated thing than our popular conceptions would have us believe. Nonetheless it is the popular conceptions built around science and its truth, which we have so internalised, which make it so hard for us to understand or even conceive alternative forms of truth.

Ironically it is the literalist reader of Scripture, either fervent believer or total disbeliever, who is the one most shaped by the populist scientific framework of the world for to both truth in Scripture is reduced to facts which are either held true or dismissed. Each will hold that the biblical creation story (there are actually two) must be factually true or it is false. The believing literalist will defend the story to the death for if it is not literally true than the whole edifice of the Bible, faith etc. will fall, for truth must be absolute not falsifiable at any point for with one brick removed all will be caused to collapse, while likewise the sceptic, believing they have proved the biblical creation story wrong, likewise believes that by showing this story to be false they have shown that the whole biblical and faith edifice has collapsed. The fundamentalist and Richard Dawkins reside close together!

We extend this limited 'scientific' understanding into many other disciplines in an attempt to turn them into factual 'sciences' so as to give them greater credibility thereby enabling us, we believe, to prove statements made within them to be either factually true or false, by their imitation of science. Thus, the attempt of such humanities as sociology and psychology to become social 'sciences.' The 'history wars' likewise represent another attempt at claiming factual truth where one view of history is seen to be correct with others being seen to be necessarily false.

Even in the arts we seek a true factual understanding of what is been said or has been produced. The visual artist or poet is then pestered with questions as to what their piece means and what is its correct interpretation, an interpretation which will then necessarily exclude all others as false. This of course is to not appreciate the art piece for essentially the artist is attempting to speak a deeper truth than one which can be simply objectified. Rather than speaking merely to such surface concern good art forms create meanings which speak to our deep inner essence of being and experience, and the more deeply they do so the more profoundly true that piece of art is said to be. The deeper truth of myth is best equated with just how we recognize that the truth in a piece of art, poetry or music extends far beyond the factual brushstrokes or ink in the form of notes or letters on paper. Likewise, the meaning of myth extends far beyond the objectifiable and quantifiable.

Both Beethoven and I could write a piece of music technically correct therefore 'factually true' as being 'music' but it is highly improbable my piece would speak to the same deep place of truth within us as would his. Likewise, both Picasso and I can fill a canvas but again it is improbable that my piece will speak to us the truth evident in his work. Yet both he and I will have created something factually called 'art.' If art or music is measured in factual truth, then neither Beethoven nor Picasso are in any way superior in their fields than me. Indeed, in objectively presenting a woman's figure my piece is likely to bear more resemblance than Picasso's to the objective factual female anatomy.

1: A myth is not a lie

Essentially, of course their works, and even mine, are not attempts at factual truth as though you would think any figure either of us draws has actual sentient being or that you will say sell your house to live instead within that 'house' which we may paint on canvas. Rather these works are an attempt at what best be described as existential truth, at drawing us to deep inner questioning about ourselves, our world and our place within that world. The ability to profoundly raise such questions, as I have noted, is usually what separates good art from that which is not, even if the latter be very well technically executed. We could of course likewise speak of any of the art forms; poetry, writing, dance or film among others. Like art, myth when it is most effective, speaks those deep existential questions to us and in so doing provides meaning, direction and purpose for life.

The truth of Christmas likewise is not a factual one as I shall show. Its truth lies, as with the arts, in another deeper domain, a domain which precludes it being proved or disproved by the historical veracity of the events in the story. Its 'truth' lies in myth. To put it plainly I am arguing that almost all the Christmas story is simply not factually or historically true but possesses deep truth in another way. Within the story there is a kernel of factual truth but that has been overlaid with a large amount of myth, magic and legend. Further the limited factual truth contained within the stories is not the key to their meaning. A factual truth found in the Lukan story tells us that Augustus was emperor at the time of the birth of Jesus, but we do not read and celebrate the stories for that factual truth. The truth of the stories lies rather in the myth, magic and legend built around and over these factual points. If we are to arrive at the truth of Christmas we need not to try and prove the factuality of the incredible events described in the gospel accounts, which of course in reality most of us can't believe, but instead to move past these to the underlying meaning. We need to de-mythologise the story and to do that paradoxically we need to understand the myths used in the stories and what those myths symbolise, for in understanding these lies the key to comprehending the deeper things to which they point.

In our examining myth let us now look more specifically at myth as used in Scripture. We will commence by turning to an example of myth with which we will no doubt be familiar; the story of Adam and Eve. Here is a classical myth for the ancient Hebrews. In this story, we are clearly in that realm of myth for no one today, except the most literal of fundamentalists, would take the story literally or factually. Indeed, the name Adam simply means 'humanity' while Eve means 'life'. If not providing us with a literal account of the genesis of humanity what then do the stories (there are two) in Genesis, do? What are their purpose?

Primarily these stories seek to give reason for human estrangement with God and the entry of evil into our world. In wrestling with this core question, the text is a response to such questions as: Why did the writers as human beings feel estrangement from God? Why were they so conscious of their wrong-doing? How did evil enter a world perfectly created, as indeed it had to be, by a perfect God? What was the nature of human free will and did it necessarily have to turn to wrong-doing? All these profound questions are caught up in this creation myth. In attempting to give reason for these things the myth also speaks of other things. Thus, in the creation story we find the place of human beings over the rest of creation including the place of the animal kingdom, this placement raising many important questions in light of the modern ecological crisis. The story also gives explanation and/or justification for the dominance of men over women. If it is giving explanation only it is serving primarily to give a reasoning for a fact as observed by ancients of that time, that indeed males were now the dominant gender, though there are questions as to whether that had always been the case. If the myth is however giving justification for such ordering, and I believe it is, then it has moved into the realm of ideology. Ideology, as I am using it here, is the deliberate use of myth in the service of self-interest, here the self-interest of the male biblical writers. Myth also represents an attempt to make sense or give explication of the strange things which we observe in life and in this they operate in more innocent ways by seeking to explain the sorts of queries that may fascinate us. Thus, here the question of the rib cage and the supposedly differing number of ribs for men and women is addressed and likewise the story seeks to give reason for the strange nature of the snake being a creature lacking legs.

Of course, the Adam and Eve story is not meant to be factually true. We all clearly know of many cases where a man has been born of a woman. I would hazard a guess that none of us know of the obverse, a woman born out of man! The story clearly reverses a biological reality so to either simply make a point, or here surely to give a self-interested ideological justification for male dominance. Further, I would hazard a guess also that none of us have ever witnessed a snake speaking, never mind arguing theology! When put as such it is clear to all but the most rigid fundamental literalist that the stories are not to be understood factually.

Indeed, the whole story is framed by myth, this search for explication. At several points it draws on older myths from surrounding cultures. The image of the tree, or in this story the two trees of life and the knowledge of good and evil, is found as 'axis mundi' or world centre in myths right around the world, while the snake linked with wisdom, though in this story a perverted type of wisdom, has in like manner a very ancient domain. Those neighbours to Israel, the Assyrians were known as the 'people mad about trees' while the snake as archetypal symbol is found everywhere from my homeland, Australia as 'rainbow serpent', to South East Asia, Central America and of course the Middle East among others. One obvious and most interesting comparison is to note how these two symbols, tree and snake serve an integral part, in a very different way, in the genesis of another great religion; Buddhism. There, in contrast to the Judeo-Christian story, both are viewed positively with the Buddha finding enlightenment under the Bodhi tree protected by the snake. In that story, the attempt of a human being to become as a god, or indeed to move beyond the gods, is viewed positively as the acquisition of wisdom while in the Genesis creation account the attempt to become wise as God is understood negatively as human hubris.

Myth is crucially important and it's power can be shown in how in this mythical story are set in place two massive assumptions that down the ages have been just taken as 'given;' men's dominance over women and human dominance over the rest of creation, understood as existing for our service. These 'natural' assumptions, drawn from this core myth of Western civilization, have had a massive effect on Western self-understanding. Only in the last fifty years or so have these so called 'natural' assumptions come to be questioned. That they held sway as 'natural' givens for so long shows the profound power that is in myth! Clearly myth has a truth and power of its own, entirely separate from factual truth, equally powerful if not even stronger. This can be seen in the oft quoted line, 'Don't confuse me with facts. My mind is made up.' Usually it is myth, often used as ideology, that has caused the mind to be made up, and no amount of factual evidence is unable to undo that made up mind.

What are we do then with myth? The German 20th century theologian Rudolf Bultmann, primarily known for his theological project of demythologising the scriptures, noted invoking the technology of the time, 'We cannot use electric lights and radios and, in the event of illness, avail ourselves of modern medicine and clinical means and at the same time believe in the spirit and wonder world of the New Testament.' [3] We even more so can't just take literally the myths entwined in the text for now Bultmann's radios and electric lights have been replaced by computers, space-flight and interactive televisions. As Bultmann calls us to do we need to demythologise the Scriptures, acknowledging that myth is indeed central to them, and reading through those eyes search for the deeper place from and to whence the myths both spring and point, rather than reading through the eyes of the literalist. Only when we read the Scriptures in such manner beyond literalism will we understand them and be able to access their depth meaning. The biblical scholar John Dominic Crossan has tellingly cast it thus; we think of those who wrote the Scriptures that they wrote literally and we, being sophisticated, can read them symbolically as they are meant to be read, whereas, he charges, the truth is that they wrote them symbolically and it is we who all too often read them literally. This needing to let go of the literal truth of the stories when it comes to the Christmas story is however very difficult of course for many of us who have so fallen deeply in love with them. As John Shelby Spong notes, 'Romantic, nostalgic, unchallenged tales die hard.' [4]

Of course, as said, there will be many who will take offence at the idea that Scriptural stories may be myth and therefore not literally true, especially those stories like the Christmas accounts in which they have invested great emotional energy. Yet it must be clear that these are stories simply are not meant to be read as being literally true for no one writing 80 to 110 years (the range of dates given for the writing of Matthew and Luke's gospels) after the event would have known anything about Jesus' birth. They didn't have access to the supposed 'facts.' It is all too easy for us to sloppily assume that given the importance of Jesus in world history information about his birth would be known but this is to neglect the reality that Jesus' fame was a later acquisition and that at birth he was a peasant total unknown. In the ancient world, the events to do with the births of those from powerful families were the only births known and myths, ever more incredible, soon accumulated around them, but the events surrounding the births of those who would later become great, not because of their familial links, but rather through their own lives, were unknown as that greatness at birth was not yet present. Only later when they did become great did myths begin to accumulate around their births. Those myths had however factually nothing to do with the unknown actual reality. Jesus, and we may add Moses around whom also birth myths accumulated, are examples of this category not born great but who became great. Jesus was born into a peasant artisan family and no one would have known anything of his birth except his immediate family and kinsmen and after the length of time of which we are speaking, they would have been very thin, if at all existing, on the ground. Further given that myths soon acquired around the lives, including the births, of those who like Jesus became great in the ancient world, even if historical memories of his actual birth were remembered, they would have been overlaid with myth as indeed likewise was the case for those born great, the Alexanders and the Caesars of antiquity. Of the latter facts of actual birth would have been known but those facts were soon submerged by myths woven around their births. Myth, along with legend, in antiquity wins out over history.

Lest we should be too shocked that the gospel writers should elaborate by the using myth when they write their infancy narratives we should tellingly remember that one of the two gospel writers from whom we have an infancy narrative; Matthew, is prepared even to elaborate with myth and legend the events which lie at the very heart of the Christian story, the trial and crucifixion of Jesus. There he writes of Pilate's wife's dream, an event which could not be in any way known to him (Matthew 27:19). If Matthew can write such legend and myth around an event, the passion narrative, at the heart of the gospel, which would have already been remembered both by eyewitnesses and which was already placed into written form in the tradition, Mark's gospel being the clearest evidence of that, how much more then would he use myth and legend in his own original composition of the nativity story? I reiterate however once again, we ought not be offended when we hear the gospel stories use myth for by our examination of myth we have seen how in their use of such the evangelists are able to tell us deeper things about the writer's understanding of Jesus than a mere factual account could ever do!

A further clue to the different nature of the nativity story in Matthew's gospel can be found in how Jesus is revealed. In the rest of the gospel, as a carry-over from what scholars of Mark call the 'Markan secret,' Jesus' true identity is mostly hidden, the veil rarely being drawn aside, resulting therefore in few apprehending his identity. We often miss this as we read our gospels through the eyes of faith knowing Jesus as 'Lord and Saviour.' If we could blinker that out and read the gospel accounts without that assumption we would find just how unknowing were those who first heard Jesus concerning his identity, even those closest to him seemingly not having a clue. Jesus even seems to foster this unknowingness by refusing to reveal his identity, and on occasions when that identity is glimpsed he adjures those who know to keep silent (Matthew 8:2-4, 13:10-15, 16:13-20 et. al). [5] Yet in their nativity stories Matthew and then Luke have Jesus' identity overtly revealed in the most spectacular manner by dreams, exotic visitors, angelic choruses and even a celestial sign of a star westward proceeding. If that was the reality how could it be that later those from Jesus' hometown have no clue that there is anything special about him? To any idea that he may have greatness or a special nature about him they, instead of remembering the supposed spectacular events associated with his birth, respond indicating his absolute mundanity, 'Isn't he the carpenter's

1: A myth is not a lie

son? Don't we know his siblings?' (Matthew 13:55). If someone after all was born in my hometown, a place much bigger than that in which Jesus was born, with all those signs attached to them would I or anyone else forget that there was something great or special about them, even thirty years down the track? In short, the hidden Jesus of the rest of the gospel stands in stark contrast to the one so openly and spectacularly identified in the infancy narratives.

Of course, the writers of Scripture would not have understood our concern for factual truth for the question of truth stated in the way we have come to understand it would not have meant anything to them. They would have been more likely to say events must have happened in a manner as announced by the prophets rather than in any factual manner, even if remembered, for prophetic utterances had far greater status than mere historical memories. This is not hidden with Matthew himself making such understanding clear when in his nativity story he writes, 'all this took place to fulfil what the Lord had spoken by the prophet' (Matthew 1:22). Prophets they understood as foretelling as well as forth telling and so in their construction of the nativity stories both Matthew and Luke search the Scriptures for prophecies which they use to frame their accounts. In reading those stories we see such, time and time again. The rigorous understanding of history as an attempt to find factual truth, that with which we are familiar, is only a comparatively modern discipline. The histories of antiquity were accounts where fact was clearly mixed with legend and myth as even a cursory reading of any of them will show.

Further it is totally nonsensical to take the stories literally and I say that with such confidence precisely because of what the goal of the two stories is about. The stories are not attempts at answering factual questions concerning Jesus' birth but rather at heart are attempts theologically to answer the question of just when did Jesus become divine. In their nativity stories both Matthew and Luke seek to show that Jesus is divine not from his resurrection as Paul believed, nor from his baptism as was the belief of Mark, but rather from his birth. This immediately raises for us logically a massive conundrum. Are we to believe that as an infant, Jesus, having the fullness of divinity as well as humanity, had all the divine attributes? Were omnipotence (being all powerful), omniscience (being all seeing/knowing) omnipresence (being present in all times and places), among other divine attributes his, as he lay in the crib? What became Christian orthodoxy would assume that indeed he did for the fullness of divinity was always with Jesus. Christian orthodoxy then if carried through to its logical conclusion would have us believe that the divine infant as he lay 'awakening no crying' making would have known the nature of quantum physics and that $E=MC^2$ long before Einstein. If by chance he did know all this we may well ask how then was this birth the birth of an infant like us in every respect, something again which Christian orthodoxy demands? We could rightly ask what status do such faith statements have and what sense they make. Of course, this theological stringency is to ask too much of the stories which, even though they themselves are framed by theological parameters, are essentially mythological creations. If the stories however were to be understood literally such questioning would be in order. Being myth, they are of course clearly not to be so understood.

The stories then, full of myth have the goal of making the theological point that in Jesus the fullness of divinity is present and that it has been present always with him from birth. John in seeking to make sense of Jesus' divinity, pushes that divinity further back making Jesus the 'Word,' the ever-present divine force through which God had created, which in the fullness of time became realized or made present in Jesus (John 1:1-18). Jesus states John whether at his resurrection, baptism or birth never acquired divinity but instead had always been divine as the eternal Word. This would seem to represent a more sophisticated answer to Jesus' divinity and having done that the writer of the prologue of John sees no need to use the Christmas narrative traditions which by the time of his writing, his being one of the final pieces in the Christian Scripture, must have been known. This again is further evidence of the lack of status of the nativity narratives.

Before moving from myth, it is important to realize that though the modern mind often believes the power of myth is no longer present in shaping our world view with we moderns having supposedly moved on into a more rational scientific age, myth operates more strongly, and often more covertly and subtly than ever. Indeed, it's strength may well be precisely because people believe they are purely objective, shaped by the 'objective truths of science.' Given such, myth being both invisible and unacknowledged is doubly strong in its effectiveness. Thus, how often do we hear people whose views are clearly framed by myth exclaim defending that view they hold, 'but that's just common sense?' Thus, a geo-political statement is easily made such as, 'everyone knows the Chinese are an aggressive people set on taking over the world' without any reference to history which of course clearly shows the Chinese have been more sinned against than been sinners regarding invading/being invaded. What has happened in the above statement of course is that myth operating as ideology has masked itself as objective accepted truth. Myth by its provision of frameworks of meaning and doing so in the modern world so covertly, is readily available for use as ideology. Much of modern politics is about using myth as ideology for advantage. We should clearly expect that ideology was at work if such statements, as is often the case, are directed at the Chinese by a rival super-power.

Another few examples of the modern power of myth and its availability to be used as ideology will suffice. Within the land in which I live, Australia, the myth of the invading hordes from the north, which of course relates to the above example, is still something extremely powerful in framing the Australian psyche and as such is available for ideological use by any unscrupulous politician. Thus, so that myth had powerful effect in framing the general Australian response to the then Prime Minister John Howard's refugee policy in the early years of this century. In his statement 'we will determine who comes to our shores' he was playing to deep myth using it as ideology in that the deep-seated myth was used deliberately in a manipulative manner for political self-interest. By what I have said concerning the power of myth one would expect it to work very effectively for him, and it did.

The United States of America is still profoundly shaped by the mythological idea of 'manifest destiny', the idea that it must carry its enlightened values to the world. Though currently those of both the Left and the Right in that land are perhaps more strongly divided than ever before, they will both, shaped by that belief, desire to carry out that 'manifest destiny' in different styles for each is profoundly shaped by it. Myth as such is simply a 'given' rather than a thought through position. It is as though the myth speaks the person. Before leaving this topic, we may point out that the power of the Western myth of the 'evil Muslim fundamentalist' as being one that has come to have powerful resonance in the West and as such is available to be used as ideology, as of course does the narrative of the evil decadent West have strong traction in some Islamic circles as witnessed in the success of militant Islamic groups. Myth along with its use in ideological form is certainly not absent from our Scriptures.

On turning to the myths associated with Christmas we are in a veritable forest of such. The Scriptures give us many, but beyond the myths they give us in which to frame our experience of Christmas, the ongoing tradition gives us many others. Many will be surprised to learn that the stable is one of those from the non-Biblical tradition. In neither gospel account is Jesus born in a stable. Matthew explicitly tells us that the wise men entered a house where they worshipped him and gave their gifts (Matthew 1:11). The greatest legend which has become attached to Christmas is of course the date of its celebration. The Scriptures tell us nothing of the now accepted date for Christmas, December 25. They actually point away from that date for Luke's shepherds were hardly likely to be minding their flock on a hillside in the dead of winter! Why then this date? Our date was originally thought by the Romans to be the winter solstice and as such was celebrated as the Feast of Saturnalia. Given the popularity of the festival celebrating the return of the sun from its retreat into darkness it was co-opted by the church along the lines, 'if you can't beat them join them.' In setting this date the church was making use of an ancient myth and cleverly co-opting it in an ideological manner seen in it's very deliberate use of a powerful myth to push an agenda, the propagation of the faith they held and the suppression of other pagan celebrations. This co-option took place a considerable time after Jesus, indeed from a time when the empire had been 'Christianised.' Christmas, wasn't celebrated in Rome until 354, Constantinople 379, and in another important early Christian centre, Antioch, in modern day Syria, not until 388. It will no doubt shock many to see just how peripheral that festival we believe to be central to our Christian experience, was to the early church over several centuries.

Of course, new myths keep being added. That of Santa Claus, while going back to Saint Nicholas of Myra (c.280-343), only developed into his widely recognized modern form with obesity, red suit and cap some 140 years ago, with an advertising campaign of Coca Cola in the 1930s cementing that image. Rudolf the red nosed reindeer, so much part of Christmas today only goes back to 1939, while commercial interests were behind the recent advent of the Christmas card, now in the age of electronic communication facing its demise.

So, let us turn to look more closely at our Christmas story, a story we are convinced we know so well, and why, we ask shouldn't we as we have probably celebrated it from birth? If so we are in for some shocks and surprises the first being, as already intimated, that there is no single story but rather two very different accounts.

Endnotes

1 It has become increasingly common to avoid the terminology of Old Testament and New Testament as though one supersedes the other being its superior. The relegation of that Testament central to Judaism is understood as being something not entirely appropriate nor very sensitive. As an alternative, the terms Jewish or Hebrew Scriptures are used for the 'Old Testament' and Greek or Christian Scriptures are used for the 'New Testament.' In this work I shall use these alternative terms.

2 For those interested in further exploring the issue of myth I refer them to the vast corpus of works, both written and visual, of Joseph Campbell. A good beginning is the series, 'The Power of Myth' where he is interviewed by Bill Moyers. See also Joseph Campbell, The Masks of God (in three parts, Occidental, Oriental and Creative Mythology), Arkana, New York, 1968

3 Rudolf Bultmann, New Testament Mythology and Other Basic Writings, Ed. Schubert M. Ogden, Philadelphia: Fortress, 1984: 3

4 John Shelby Spong: Jesus for the Non-Religious, Harper Collins, San Francisco, 2007:15

5 William Wrede in 1901 was the first to point out how Jesus in the Gospel of Mark often commands those who understand his status as Messiah to be silent about it. That adjuring to silence carries over into the two gospels in which are found the nativity stories; Matthew and Luke. I have given Matthean examples here each of which carries straight over from the earlier parallel found in Mark's gospel. William Wrede, The Messianic Secret, London: James Clarke, 1987

2: 'The' Christmas Story?

On turning to the biblical Christmas stories after the first surprise of finding there are two quite two distinct Christmas stories hardly crossing at any point, our next may be to learn that only two of our four canonical gospels contain Christmas stories with neither Mark, the earliest gospel, nor John, containing infancy narratives. It may cause further surprise to know that our earliest Christian writings come not from one of the gospel authors, but from Paul, and he again in his epistles knows nothing of the birth tradition, although to be fair he shows little interest in any of the events to do with the life of Jesus.

So entranced have we become by the myth and magic along with familiarity of the Christmas events that we tend quite unconsciously to conflate the two Christmas stories into one. The shepherds and the wise men come to be for us in the same story and we conjecture that maybe they even met, the wise men stopping on their way for a cup of brew with the shepherds out in the fields. Of course, they don't belong in the same narrative, the shepherds belonging to one, the wise men to another. For many Christmas carols have become the means through which they perceive the story and in this regard, they are often most unhelpful. Read the words of 'The First Nowell' and there you will find a classic conflating of these two stories with both the wise men and the shepherds, we are explicitly told, following the same star.

Not only are there two nativity stories but as already said they differ on just about every point. So intertwined have they become for us we need really to read each of the accounts of Matthew and Luke with blinkers so to exclude the other. The familiarity is such however that perhaps no blinkers could suffice. Only by at least trying however will we then see for example that the wise men and the shepherds don't belong together at all being in different gospels, Matthew and Luke respectively, nor do the star westward proceeding and the celestial lights accompanied by the angelic chorus belong together, those stories again being found respectively in those two different gospel accounts.

One might then be inclined to ask why do two of our gospels have no nativity story and why do the two we have such a variance about them? Those would be fair questions if we were talking about histories, but we are not. To be fair in this the gospel writers are honest for they do not claim that they are writing historical accounts but rather gospels, pieces which are 'good news.' This is what the Old English term 'gospel' means this rendering in English being a correct translation from the Greek 'euangelion' the self-denoted term used in the gospels, written in that language. The evangel of course is one who bears good news and so correctly we should speak thus of the four evangelists, the gospel writers, which of course we do, rather than calling them historians.

Despite this open honesty in the nomenclature they both give themselves, and by what we call them we still all too often think the evangelists are writing histories. In actuality the writers of the gospels are not so much concerned to give an historical account of the life of Jesus as to change the life of us, the readers. That last sentence I invite you to read again because until one comprehends that one never will understand the purpose of the gospel writers. Only in understanding this will we be able to read the gospels in a manner by which we can access and experience their true profundity. To carry out that aim of causing an existential change in your life, your history, by encounter with the risen Christ, they present that risen Christ as Jesus walking through a constructed history. They determine what they will include in that 'history' based on what they think will be seminal in changing the reader's life and the calling of them to follow the risen Christ. Hence the differences in each gospel for each gospel writer has a distinct theology and so writes accordingly. This is not at all to say that there is no historicity to the gospels. Historical events are included but these events are not the determining factor in what gets written and how that is told. Rather, again I reiterate, the determining factor is the theology of the evangelist and how that theology shapes the story with its goal of changing the reader's life with a call then to discipleship.

As we know storytelling, when done well reaches deep recesses within us, and seemingly with that in mind our four canonical gospel writers create narrative stories which appear as history. That these stories have proved to be such an effective method of carrying out their aim in making sense of Jesus to us and allowing that understanding to change our lives shows just how well-crafted they have been. This narrative method appearing as history has been a crucial part of that success. One clear mark of that success is that despite the often-clear differences in the gospels we simply think each is telling us 'the true story of Jesus' or we simply don't notice that they vary, even on occasions being at odds with each other.

In their use of a common method of storytelling the four canonical gospel writers are different to some of the other gospels written which have not made it into the Christian Scriptures. There are of course other methods of carrying out that goal of which we have been speaking, changing readers minds and bringing them into discipleship of Jesus. Narrative is not essential to this aim though as I have just said it is a highly successful method. Another method is at work for example in a gospel which never made it into the canonical Scriptures, the Gospel of Thomas, found at Nag Hammadi, Egypt in 1945. [1] That gospel does not contain any narrative but consists rather 114 sayings of Jesus, presenting Jesus more in a manner of a teacher, very similar in many ways to the Buddha, who rather than giving you salvation shows you the way to achieve your own salvation. By not having any narrative this gospel of course contains no passion scene for it is the teachings of Jesus rather than the passion which are instrumental in giving salvation. It goes without saying that there is also no nativity story. This is a radically different style to our canonical gospels with a totally distinct methodology from that used in the writing of narrative. For this and other reasons some scholars, and the debate is enduring, assign the Gospel of Thomas a very early date of writing. It was rejected however by the developing church, though that rejection probably came as late as the 4th century.

It was assumed by many that such a gospel lacking narrative would never have been constructed by the infant church until scholars started to note something very interesting in the synoptic gospels, Matthew, Mark and Luke ('synoptic' literally meaning to be 'seen together'). It is generally accepted that both Matthew and Luke lift material from

Mark, the earliest of the gospels, but it is also noticeable that they share other material in common not found in Mark. Scholars believe that they were each using a gospel no longer extant, one they have called Q from the German 'Quelle' (source), a hypothetical gospel constructed by material found in common in Matthew and Luke not found in Mark. That gospel, in like manner to the Thomas gospel, consists of many sayings without any narrative.

As we have seen the theological concern of each evangelist and how that shapes their evangelical goal necessarily means that each gospel, canonical, non-canonical, narrative in style or otherwise, will vary. That variation is brought about by several factors, the first of which we have already touched on, that each author will have a different understanding of what is the good news, i.e. their theologies will vary. Second, the geographical locale and the community from out of which they write will have a significant effect on what they produce, this being because each gospel writer writes as a redactor, a final editor pulling together disparate oral and written traditions from the community within which they reside, sometimes using traditions and materials peculiar to that community. Third, the time in which they write is crucial and I will spend more time with this as it impacts greatly on what we are examining. Mark's gospel particularly is very much shaped by that cataclysmic event which so challenged Jewish understanding; the destruction of the holy city, Jerusalem and its magnificent temple in the Roman crushing of the Jewish revolt (66-70 CE), an event almost contemporaneous with the writing of that gospel. [2] That event also greatly shapes the first of our gospels containing a nativity story; Matthew.

Matthew writes some 15 years after Mark, a time when Judaism was radically re-understanding itself, the destruction of the holy city and temple making that an urgent necessity. That cataclysmic event was one which called into radical questioning the whole Jewish raison d'être, for the destruction of the holy city, and particularly that institution which lay at the heart of Jewish understanding, the temple, represented a total catastrophe for the Jewish populace. Under the leadership primarily of Johann ben Zakkai Jewish faith became radically reformed with the foundations for the type of rabbinic Judaism, which we know today, radically different from that which preceded it, being laid. Judaism became the religion of the book centred on the Torah, particularly halakhah, best understood as ethical living before God, instead of the old sacrificial system centred on cult, ritual and the Temple. Such a radical reformation must necessarily of course assert that is represents the true inheritor of a tradition from which it has radically deviated.

All this means then that the Judaism of Matthew's time of writing was very different to that in which Jesus had lived. Indeed, no faith has probably more radically been altered in such a short time than the Judaism of that epoch. Because of the cataclysmic change brought about by the Temple's destruction most of the Jewish schools of thought present at the time of Jesus no longer therefore existed during the time of the Matthew's writing following the Roman reconquest.

We need to briefly examine these schools present at the time of Jesus and what happened to them. The first of these, the Sadducees, were representative of the temple establishment and its sacrificial system. They were essentially conservative holding only to the Torah (the first five books of the Hebrew Scripture; the Law) and rejecting what they considered to be newer writings and traditions. Thus, they did not believe, as we read even in our gospels of such a 'new-fangled' idea as life after death (Matthew 22:23). The Sadducees so central to Jewish life in the time of Jesus, by time Matthew's time of writing, being so identified with the Temple, now destroyed, no longer given that link, had any place. The second group, the Essenes, were a group understanding themselves as a new purified temple establishment and are best known by the Qumran community built on an escarpment above the Dead Sea, the place in which were found the Dead Sea Scrolls. The Essenes were ardent nationalists with one of their documents 'the War Scroll' speaking of an apocalyptic battle between the forces of righteousness as represented by them, and the forces of evil, the 'kittim', a name which it is believed alluded to the Romans. Though the battle would be won primarily through divine intervention rather than their own part the Essenes were considered sufficiently rebellious to be crushed under Roman might. The third group were the Zealots, political rebels who having been utterly crushed like the Essenes, likewise were left with their central narrative in ruins, the result being that they also were marginalised during the time of the gospel writings. I say marginalised only because they would rise again in the Bar Kockba revolt against Rome 132-135 CE. The fourth group, the Pharisees were the group most popular at the time of Jesus but held little political power, their popularity perhaps being precisely a result of their not being involved in the Jewish political order and its collaboration with the occupying Romans. As fellowships built around various teachers the Pharisees sought to extend the codes of purity, originally given in the Torah and the oral tradition for the priests and Levites, to all the Jewish population with the goal of creating a holy nation worthy of being God's people. They were the group best suited to survive the cataclysm of the Roman destruction and it is from this group we find the seeds of the rabbinic Judaism of which I have spoken.

Before we move from here we must disavow ourselves of the ideas that we naturally associate with the term 'pharisee'; narrow mindedness, oppressiveness, and bigotry. If these ideas typified their being it is unlikely that they would have been held in the high esteem in which we know they were. That we hold such an understanding of them is precisely because of the success of the Matthean (ideological) theological project and it is to this project I now turn.

Along with the mainstream Jewish reform under Johannan ben Zakkai leading to rabbinic Judaism, there was another group which sought to assert that it was the true fruit of the old, now destroyed, tradition. They also were creating something radically different from that tradition they were now claiming as their own. This group from within the Jewish community were followers of Jesus, whom I will call the 'Jesus Jews.' Matthew is representative of this group who argued that Jesus had come as the Messiah to fulfil the Jewish expectation but had done so in a radically different manner to that commonly expected. That these 'Jesus Jews' were only a small proportion of the Jewish community is to be expected when one considers just how far Jesus was from fulfilling the commonly accepted Jewish messianic expectation. Essentially put Matthew's theological project is to show that it is this group of 'Jesus Jews', not the renewed rabbinic Judaism initiated under ben Zakkai,, who represent the true inheritance of the Jewish tradition.

Given this Matthean project those majority Jews reforming themselves into rabbinic Judaism following the demise of the Temple cult with the Roman destruction during the 66-70 CE rebellion, are viewed very negatively in this gospel as they increasingly turned a blind eye to the message concerning Jesus. That they were turning away, indeed reacting against what they understood as the ever increasing 'heresies' being practiced by the Jesus Jews is of course entirely understandable. It is the normal reaction of a community under threat or worse desperately seeking what could be called identity survival, following the disasters of the failed rebellion, to turn the wagons into a defensive circle. Further how after-all could this Jesus be the Messiah, when instead of bringing liberation to Israel he had been taken by the Romans and shamefully executed with the method of execution, upon a tree, being one which only the cursed suffered (Deuteronomy 21:23)? How could he be the Messiah when so soon after his life such total catastrophe had beset the Jewish nation? Further now this movement had begun to accept gentiles, the same people who had just destroyed the holy temple, into their circle sometimes without their needing even to adhere to the Torah or indeed to undergo that which most distinguished the Jewish people; circumcision. All this served to drive the wedge further between the two groups.

Essentially both groups, rabbinic Judaism and the Jesus Jews, each of them very different from the sacred tradition from which they had come, were making competing claims to that tradition from which they each so differed, seeking to legitimise themselves through it.

For Matthew to present his community as the true inheritors of the tradition he then gives us a Jesus standing very firmly in the sacred tradition, one who is very strict in following and even tightening the strictures of the Torah. We see such a figure in the Sermon on the Mount where several times Jesus says, 'You have heard it said.... but now I say to you,' each time tightening the strictures of the Law (Matthew 5:20-48). This Matthean Jesus charges that, 'not an iota of the Law will be done away with while heaven and earth last' (Matthew: 5:18-19). We can compare this Jesus to that of Paul where it is claimed that following him the Law, being a guardian from which we now have outgrown, no longer has standing (Galatians 3:24).

Given that the successors of the Pharisees, the emerging rabbinic Judaism represented the main competition to the community of Jesus Jews, it was inevitable that Matthew would place retrospectively that current opposition between his community and rabbinic Judaism onto Jesus and the predecessors of the rabbis, the Pharisees. Thus, the Jesus of Matthew's account being presented therefore as one continually in opposition to the Pharisees, whereas it is likely in his actual lifetime he was probably most identified with this grouping. Even a cursory reading of Matthew's gospel will out the truth by showing that Jesus was primarily mixing with the Pharisees and it is with them that his teaching style and method most approximate. Like them he has a fellowship around him, preaches a transforming holiness to all, intensifies the strictures of the Law, and is often involved in table gatherings; all things distinctive of the Pharisees.

The result is that Matthew is the most Jewish gospel in that it claims for the nascent Jesus movement the ancient Jewish tradition, but the most anti-Jewish in that the contemporary Jewish faith of his time is rejected with that rejection then being cast back upon the very different context in which Jesus ministered so to have a Jesus in deep conflict with the contemporary representatives of his own faith tradition.

This anti-Jewish agenda of Matthew of course enters also into his nativity story and we will see it at work several times. Thus, in Matthew's gospel in a perverse reversal of the Exodus story the holy family must flee from evil in Israel, of course identified in Matthew's mind with the renewed rabbinic Judaism, to find sanctuary in Egypt. They must flee not because of the actions of a foreign king as long ago in their past with Pharaoh's actions, but rather because of those of a Jewish king, never mind that Herod was hardly the paragon of Jewish piety or indeed even Jewish! He will do however to represent the Jewish opposition to the gospel. To make the point even more strongly Herod's rejection is contrasted with the pious worship of gentile foreigners; the three wise men.

2: 'The' Christmas Story?

Matthew as we have seen is one of the two canonical gospels in which we find an infancy narrative. The other is Luke so let us turn now to that gospel and to Luke's agenda.

The dating of Luke's gospel raises many questions, different scholars placing it as early as Matthew's gospel, around 85 CE, while others place it as late as 110 CE. Luke is possibly, the only non-Jewish writer in the Christian Scriptures, though this also is hotly debated. His prime agenda is to move the Christian faith as far away as possible from the rebellious roots which had led to the Jewish uprising thereby presenting a gospel which fits respectably into the surrounding milieu, particularly of course the Roman social and political system. In this he, like Matthew, takes his current theological agenda and casts it back retrospectively to the time of Jesus and his ministry, his theological agenda however being very different from that of his fellow gospel writer. Whereas Matthew shows Jesus in conflict with his tradition Luke presents a Jesus sitting much more comfortably in that tradition which spawned him. In like manner the nascent Christian church sits comfortably within the Empire.

Luke commences his gospel making the claim of historical veracity with an almost backhanded dismissal of other accounts, 'Since many have undertaken to compile a narrative....it seemed good for me also, having followed all things closely....to write an orderly account (Luke 1:1-3). By so doing Luke goes as near as we get in the gospels to calling factual history to his side. Despite this claim to historical veracity at the commencement of his gospel he however then immediately launches into a Christmas story, a story, like that of Matthew, owing very little to actual historical events! Luke, like Matthew, could have known nothing of course of the actual events surrounding Jesus' birth especially so given that he is writing later again. As in the case of Matthew it is a theological rather than an historical concern which shapes his construction of the nativity story. Luke's theological project as already identified, is however very distinct from that of Matthew. Thus, in Luke's account there is no tyrannical king and therefore need for the family of Jesus to flee in fear of their lives, but rather a very natural integration of Jesus into his Jewish tradition. Jesus is twice taken to that place lying at the heart of the Jewish established order, the Temple being presented to the priests so to fulfil the usual customs with his status being affirmed most strongly by two aged figures, one of each gender, Simeon (Luke 2:25-35) and Anna (Luke 2:36-38) who by their age represent of course continuity with the tradition. That continuity with the tradition is again present later when Jesus and the family go up to the temple when he is twelve years old. So well does Jesus fit into his Jewish faith tradition he remains there we are told learning from the elders (Luke 2:41-50).

The Christmas stories of both Matthew and Luke then, while they appear to be historical accounts especially in that their use of narrative form, the form in which history is written, are really anything but factual accounts of historical events. It need be said that while the Christmas stories invade history and make use of historical categories and figures such as Caesar, Herod the Great and Quirinius that does not make them historical. As has been elsewhere expressed the legends and myths of Robin Hood also make use of historical figures and events, the crusades, the Sheriff of Nottingham and King Richard, but such usage does not those legends and myths historical. [3]

Lest there be objection to my questioning the historical veracity of the nativity accounts it need be pointed out that such questioning of the truth of the Christmas stories is not a recent phenomenon but rather has been happening for a long time, indeed from shortly after the time of their composition. As early as 178 CE the pagan philosopher Celsus attacked the Christmas stories charging that they were concoctions designed to cover up Jesus being the illegitimate son of Mary with a Roman legionary. The Jewish Talmud likewise charges that Jesus is the son of Mary and a Roman soldier, Panthera. [4] While the Talmud is a late 4-5th century writing it has roots in earlier Jewish tradition no doubt reflective of how many of the local Jewish populace, contemporary with the gospel writers, may have viewed the Christian claims. It should be pointed out there is no compelling evidence for these charges however for Jesus was a very common name with the contemporary Jewish historian Josephus listing several, meaning that it is impossible to prove the Jesus or Yeshua, of Christianity is Yeshua ben (son of) Panthera. There are even four men named Jesus in the Jerusalem Temple's line of 28 priests! Further the name Panthera may not even reflect a real person but could easily be one conveniently made up in a caustic ironical manner from the Greek parthenos meaning virgin, that being an incorrect translation, as we shall see, from the Hebrew of the passage in Isaiah (7:14) from where clearly Matthew develops his idea of the virgin birth. This we shall explore further.

Let us turn then to those two infancy narratives we have in Matthew and Luke and lay them beside each other for comparison. When we do so we will find that those two stories we have, so full of myth, magic and legend, hardly concur on any point.

MATTHEW	LUKE
The genealogy	Birth of John the Baptist foretold
The virginal conception of Jesus	The annunciation to Mary
Joseph's first dream	The visitation of Mary to Elizabeth
The birth of Jesus	The Magnificat
The wise men and Herod	Birth and circumcision of John the Baptist
Visit of the wise men	The Benedictus
Joseph's second dream	Census and journey to Bethlehem
The journey into Egypt	The birth of Jesus
Massacre of the innocents	The Shepherds
Intends to return to Bethlehem	Jesus' Circumcision and purification
after Herod's death	Simeon and Anna's testimony
but Herod's son on throne so	Return to Nazareth
following Joseph's third dream	Jesus in the temple aged twelve
the family move to Nazareth	John the Baptist's ministry
	Jesus baptised by John
	The genealogy (given as Jesus commences his ministry)

As earlier said, when laid out thus it may come as a surprise if not a shock to most to see that the two very different stories never cross on any point with every event in each of them finding no real parallel in the other! There are a few obvious commonalities at the basic level but nothing else. What are the basic commonalities?

- Both Matthew and Luke give us the names of Jesus' parents as being Joseph and Mary with each affirming that Joseph was not the real father.
- Each gospel tells us that they were betrothed at the time of Jesus' birth.
- Both gospels claim Jesus has a Davidic descent although they lay different emphases on that descent.
- There is an annunciation by an angel in each, to Joseph in Matthew but to Mary in Luke.
- The angelic message is common in both gospels, that Mary will conceive by the Holy Spirit and that the child's name is to be Jesus.
- Both writers understand Jesus as being the light to the world by each having celestial lights associated with his birth, the star followed by the wise men in Matthew and in Luke the light associated with the angelic chorus to the shepherds. Later the early church would use this idea of light coming into the world to place Christmas at the time of the winter solstice from which point new light streams into the world.
- Matthew and Luke are both also keen to each give us a chronological line for Jesus as found in the genealogies they each give
- Each present Mary as a virgin, though this is far more emphasised, as we shall see, in Matthew than in Luke.
- Both have Bethlehem as the place of birth, varying however completely in how they get the birth to be there.
- Theologically essentially, they have in common that they are each trying to tell us that what happened in the birth of Jesus is not something simply 'of the flesh' but rather something uniquely 'of God' both understanding that in this birth and subsequent life of

the one of whom they speak something is happening which is God's greatest action, and the event on which the whole of history turns. The Divine in both stories is thus shown to have entered history in a radically new and more profound manner than ever before. Prior to this the voice of God had been heard as being present (Isaiah 55:11) but now the Divine one not merely the divine voice is shown to be present.

These are the major themes of the two nativity stories but in how those major themes are spelled out in the stories constructed there is virtually no commonality between the two gospels.

As we have seen the stories vary largely because at their heart is a different agenda around how each has Jesus relating to his surrounding milieu that being based on how each believes the faith they hold fits into its surrounding milieu. Thus, so the Jesus Matthew gives us is one at total odds with his contemporaries for they are representative of a sacred tradition, which Jesus strenuously keeps, now gone bad while the Jesus of Luke on the other hand fits hand in glove to his tradition as Luke's goal is apologetic, claiming that of this Christian movement, with clearly seditious roots, Rome need have no fear. Thus, to show how Christianity can be accommodated within the Roman Empire Luke gives us a Jesus who sits comfortably within his own community. This placing of Jesus within or in opposition to his community plays a huge part in how each evangelist has shaped the two nativity stories which we are now to examine in detail.

We shall commence with that which comes before even our stories' beginning; the ancestors.

Endnotes

1 What are commonly called the 'Gnostic Gospels' were found at Nag Hammadi, Egypt by a shepherd in 1945. Mostly the writings are clearly later gospels all bearing the marks, as their name informs, of Gnostic influence. As such they are dismissed as telling us anything of the life and teaching of Jesus, the exception being the Gospel of Thomas, which while there is divided opinion, some scholars understand, in its earlier layers as going back into the first century. These are accessible in many translations and can even be found online.

2 The accepted way of dating today has increasingly become C.E. (the Common Era) and B.C.E. (Before the Common Era), the supposed dating of Jesus' birth being still, however, the dividing line

3 A.N. Wilson: Jesus, Flamingo, London, 1993:75-76

4 Following the destruction of the second temple, that contemporaneous with Jesus, Judaism, as we have seen, radically re-oriented itself to becoming a people of the book. The Mishnah (literally 'the repeating') was the first result of this. It served as a compendium of Jewish religious tradition, rulings and commentary. This was an early second century compilation. The Talmud (literally 'study') was a further development of this same tradition. It brings together commentary on both the Mishnah and the Gemara, the latter being another compendium of teaching. There are two Talmuds, one originating from Jerusalem, the Talmud Yerushalmi (4th century C.E.), the other in Babylon, the Talmud Bavli (4-5th centuries C.E.). The latter is the more important. That the traditions, rulings and commentary accumulate can be seen in that the Talmud consists of some 6,200 pages!

3: The Family Tree

One common feature both nativity stories share is that each contain genealogies, yet as we shall see the content of both is radically different. It is with these genealogies I wish to commence our examination of the Christmas narratives. Lest such a beginning point induce a feeling of slumber, or a let's just skip this bit to those of us not highly enamoured in tracing the family tree, I hope it is sufficient here to say that each of these genealogies tell us a great deal about who both Matthew and Luke understand Jesus to be.

These genealogies found in our two gospels do not represent the first used in the Scriptures. We find that with the use of a genealogy very early in the giving of the descendants of Adam (Genesis 5) and following there are several other genealogies given in the Hebrew Scriptures. This is to be expected as such replicates the common use of genealogies in the Middle East. These genealogies were not designed to act as straight forward historical records but rather were commonly used for political or religious purposes all being compiled to meet the changing circumstances of rulers. The result is that different versions often existed side by side serving different interests, as is the case in our gospels, without any sense of incompatibility. The giving of these genealogies in both our gospels has as its purpose not historical accuracy but rather something far deeper, to establish in Jesus a new genesis or beginning, while placing him firmly in the line of the faith tradition. That these genealogies vary in actual content in carrying out that goal shows that both authors, Matthew and Luke, understand Jesus, as we have already seen, fitting in a different manner and place within that tradition.

An immediate difference we will note when comparing the genealogies is their placement for while Matthew commences his gospel by giving us the genealogy of Jesus, Luke waits to give his until just before the commencement of Jesus' ministry (Matthew 1: 1-17 c.f. Luke 3: 23-38). We will also quickly notice that while Matthew works forward chronologically from Abraham to Jesus, Luke opts to work backwards beginning with Jesus and finishing not with Abraham but rather with Adam. On further comparing these genealogies it takes again but a cursory look to find that there is almost nothing in common between the names given in the two. Noting these differences in the genealogies is nothing new for as long ago as 1490 Annius of Viterbo pointed this out, his reasoning being that Matthew takes Jesus' genealogy through Joseph, this being, he posited, the legal genealogy, while Luke takes his through Mary, the maternal genealogy. For the genealogical differences in comparing the two genealogies we only need to go back to Jesus' grandfather, given by Matthew as Jacob and Luke as Heli, to note the inconsistency. Between the time of David and that of Jesus, some ten centuries, only Zerubbabel and Shealtiel are found in both the lineages given! This is seemingly because Matthew chooses only to follow sources from the Hebrew Scriptures from Abraham to Zerubbabel before using another unknown source which does not at all tally with Luke.

In taking his genealogy back to Abraham Matthew takes us back to the genesis of the Jewish nation for to him Jesus represents primarily a new Israel. We have of course already seen how Matthew understands the community gathered around Jesus as the true inheritors of the Jewish tradition, therefore a new Israel, in opposition to the reformed rabbinic Jewish community. In Luke, on the other hand, we are taken back further, to the genesis of the whole of humanity in Adam for to Luke Jesus represents the beginning not just of Israel, but of a new humanity. A further difference is that while Matthew in his lineage emphasises the Davidic descent of Jesus understanding his being the king Messiah, Luke emphasises the priestly line of Jesus' descent viewing him as the priestly Messiah. From what we have seen of both Matthew and Luke this is entirely understandable. Matthew with a genealogy of Jesus shaped by his Jewish concern therefore emphasises Jesus' Davidic descent along with the genesis of his lineage being in Abraham understood as the genesis of the Jewish nation, differs from Luke who with his stronger universal gentile concern has Jesus' lineage going back to Adam, the ancestor of all nations, and places less emphasis on Jesus being king in the tradition of the great Jewish nationalist king, David. These are the

3: The Family Tree

broad brushstrokes however and as we shall see in closer examination a universalist interest is not entirely foreign to Matthew nor conversely is a narrower Davidic interest absent from Luke.

In post exilic Judaism, the time following the exile to Babylon from which the Jewish people had returned in 521 BCE, genealogies became an ever more important part of the Jewish understanding of the expected Messiah and a number were constructed and it is probable that either one or both of Matthew and Luke adapted their genealogies from such Jewish messianic genealogies. [1] It is a series of these post-exilic genealogies contained in the first three chapters of 1 Chronicles, which most influences both Matthew and Luke. Matthew particularly follows one of the genealogies found there, though with three generations being missed after 'the wife of Uzziah.' There are two Uzziah's mentioned in the line found in 1 Chronicles; Uzziah, Joash, Amaziah and then Uzziah so it appears that a mistake has been made in that the eye of the gospel writer slipped from one Uzziah to the other, an example of an ellipsis, or it may be that in order to follow his schema of three lots of 14 generations in his genealogy Matthew has deliberately made the alteration. Such historical inaccuracy to fit the schema may be quite intentional because, as we have seen, factual accuracy is not the point of ancient genealogies found in our Scriptures and elsewhere in antiquity. The schema, rather than history, could thus take precedence.

The differences in the genealogical lines of Matthew and Luke are particularly found after David. For Matthew, the line from David is drawn through one of his sons, Solomon, while for Luke it is drawn through another, Nathan. There is no record of Nathan though it is quite possible David had a son so called if he was giving issue through 300 wives! Alternatively, Luke either was confused mistakenly identifying a prophet of David's son Solomon's time as being an actual son, or possibly his naming of Nathan was deliberate, even if no record of such a son existed, for he knew that by not taking the genealogy through Solomon he could avoid taking it through Jehoiakim and Jehoiachin, the last two legitimate kings of Judea, of whom the prophet Jeremiah had said would have no descendants (Jeremiah 36:30).

Let us turn first to examine Matthew's genealogy in more detail. Matthew gives his genealogy in three epochs, Abraham to David, David to the exile, and from the exile to Jesus with supposedly there being 14 figures in each epoch though the last, possibly mistakenly, has only 13 although maybe Matthew is informing us that Christ as representing something totally new cannot be placed among the old and therefore must be categorised separately thereby deliberately leaving us with just 13 names in the final epoch. Elsewhere after all he tells us that the new wine cannot be contained in the old wine bags (Matthew 9:17). Again, it is possible that Matthew wishes us to understand that there are actually 14 names in the third section of his genealogy as it culminates with 'Jesus.... who is called the Christ'; i.e. given two names to both indicate his being greater than the others named and to also turn the 13 names into 14. Within the genealogy it is also possible to see these figures as representing two lots of seven in each section, seven being representative of wholeness as seen in the seventh day, the Shabbat or Sabbath being symbolic of the completeness of the creation to come in the Messianic epoch. We would have then three sections of course, with the two lots of seven in each section being then multiplied by the three giving us six which means then that Christ comes as the seventh representing the Sabbath at the culmination of a new creation. This playing with numbers however can only be conjectural though at a basic level at least such seems to be part of Matthew's schema. Numerology was important in the world of antiquity and is certainly not absent from the Scriptures.

In this numerical vein, we may note that Matthew perhaps is also playing with the numerical values given to Hebrew letters, a technique called gematria. He makes much of the Davidic descent of Jesus and in David's name we again have the number fourteen which is of course double the sacred number seven. In Hebrew, only the consonants are written with the vowels being assumed. Thus, David would have been written DVD. The value of these Hebrew consonants in the name David ($D = 4$, $V = 6$ and $D = 4$) adds thus to fourteen. The Davidic ideal, as we have already seen, is central to Matthew's understanding of Jesus.

3: The Family Tree

The Messiah it was widely believed would come out of the line of David and the Davidic ideal was strongly expressed in the tradition (Psalm 89:3-4, 132:11-12 et.al). That Jesus was understood by Matthew as the 'son of David' can be seen by the repetitive use of the term in Matthew's gospel (Matthew 1:1, 1:20, 9:27, 12:23, 15:22, 20:30, 31, 21:9, 15, 22:42, 45). Such concern is however not absent from Luke who tells us that God will give to Jesus 'the throne of his father David (Luke 1:32), while also telling us that Jesus will be born in David's city (Luke 2:4,11). Further we also have the claim made that because he was one of David's descendants Jesus was made king (Acts 2:30). That last reference of course is a Lukan context, Luke and Acts being written by the same author. This Davidic lineage will be central in determining where our two gospel writers will have Jesus born as we shall see.

We may note here two things, the first being that Jesus, himself, made little of his Davidic descent (Matthew 22: 41-45), the second being that while in the near contemporary Dead Sea scrolls it was believed that there would be a coming of two messiahs, one of the kingly line of David, the other of the priestly line of Aaron, it was the latter which was far more important.

As well as the Davidic emphasis, we find also in Matthew's genealogy a link made between Abraham and Jesus. The genealogy of Jesus commences, as we have noted, with Abraham who was understood as the father of the Jewish people, the one in whom the nation had been founded. By this concentration on Abraham and David Matthew emphasises that in Jesus and made present in his followers a new Israel is being founded with Jesus come to be its king. Again, we are reminded of Matthew's theological project to assert his community, rather than the reforming Judaism, as being the true inheritors of the sacred tradition.

Yet, despite his concern for the narrow nationalist project Matthew also has a wider more universal concern which we shall now examine. While as we have observed seemingly that Matthew's genealogy going back only to Abraham rather than Luke's Adam means that Matthew's schema is less universal being limited only to Judaism, it is important to remember that while Israel was founded in Abraham as its father he was also understood as the one through whom 'all the nations of the earth bless themselves' (Genesis 22:18, Genesis 12:3 c.f. Galatians 3:8). Therefore, Matthew is perhaps also claiming that in Jesus likewise all nations shall be blessed. To further explore this universal concern, we need first go on a short excursus.

At the time of Jesus many Jewish people lived outside Israel in what is called the 'diaspora' (emigration or dispersal). Over time many of these people lost their fluency in Hebrew speaking instead primarily the lingua-franca of the ancient Mediterranean world; Greek. The Greek they used was not classical or high Greek but rather a popular form of Greek we call 'koine' or common Greek. This simplified Greek enabled those who lacked a common native tongue to communicate somewhat like English, today's lingua-franca, is often used in a simplified form by those today lacking a common native tongue. This lack of facility with the Hebrew language by many Jews meant that it had become necessary to translate the Hebrew Scriptures into Greek in order that the Jews of the diaspora could still access them. This Greek translation of the Jewish Scriptures we know as the Septuagint or LXX, that symbol indicating that it was believed that the translation was carried out in 70 days by 70 scholars and it was this translation, rather than that in the original Hebrew, which was the text with which most diaspora Jews were most familiar. Scholars generally view the writers of the gospels, similarly lacking fluency in Hebrew, as also working mainly from this Greek translation of the Hebrew Scriptures. We know this because in those passages they quote from the Jewish Scriptures it is usually very clear that they are lifting the quotation from the LXX rather than the original Hebrew. This 'koine' or common Greek was of course the language is which the Christian Scriptures were written so when they quote texts from the Septuagint it was usually done without change unless the change is intentional to make a theological point.

Thus, given that the gospel writers are using the Septuagint or LXX of the Jewish Scriptures therefore given the commonality of the language between their writings and that from where they are quoting, important parallels can be found. Thus, in the Septuagint when that initial genealogical line of which I spoke earlier, found in the Scriptures at Genesis 5:1, is given the Greek word 'genesis' is used. Given that the line given there begins with Adam, the first human it is possible to see that in using this same word, 'genesis' of Jesus (Matthew 1:18), Matthew in his genealogy is proclaiming nothing less than that in Jesus a new humanity has its genesis. Further to this the word 'genesis' used here for announcing the birth of Jesus that same word is used at the commencement of Matthew's genealogical line (Matthew 1:1). Again, by his repetition of this word Matthew is affirming that something new, nothing less than a new genesis, a new humanity, is being made present in the birth (genesis) of Jesus. That contrast between Jesus, as a new humanity and Adam, as an old humanity is of course found elsewhere in the Scriptures (Romans 5: 12-21).

Of course, Matthew's universal concern is most overtly and strongly evident in his gospel when he concludes his writing by giving us the charge of the resurrected Jesus 'to go and make disciples of all nations' (Matthew 28:18-20).

That universalist intention to include all is again perhaps seen in how within his genealogy Matthew introduces us to five women, Tamar, Rahab, Ruth, Bathsheba (the woman who had been Uriah's wife) and of course Mary. The first four of those women from the Hebrew Scriptures could be understood as morally dubious, each being suspected to be either adulterers or at least sexually promiscuous (Genesis 38:14-18, Joshua 2:1-2, 6:22-25, 2 Samuel 11:1-5, Ruth 3: 7-15). Further three of the four come from Gentile backgrounds, Rahab (Joshua 2:1, 6, 25), Ruth (Ruth 1:14, 4:10-12) while Bathsheba is mentioned unnamed here as the wife of the Hittite commander Uriah (2 Samuel 11:3). [2] Over time three of the four of these women were elevated, Tamar seen as 'righteous' (Genesis 38: 26), Rahab understood positively (Joshua 6:25, Hebrews 11: 31, James 2: 25) and Ruth becoming known, through what is probably a later addition to the book bearing her name, as the ancestor of kings including David, while concerning the fourth, Bathsheba, only David is apportioned blame in the adulterous liaison with her. That each of these women had been elevated by the time of Matthew's writing could suggest that though moral aspersions were being cast about the fifth woman he mentions; Mary, she likewise in time will be elevated out of her current morally ambiguous background associated with having conceived Jesus out of wedlock.

Again, Matthew may have had a theological agenda in his naming such dubious women. He may be saying that the reign of God, being made present on the 'wrong' side of history, is open to all including such as these. Of course, we would be wrong to concentrate solely on the wrongs of the women in the lineage for there has been well and truly enough emphasis on the sins of women in the Christian tradition without regard for those of the men, including of course in this case David himself. Still by including the women Matthew seemingly is making clear that Jesus' message can't be circumscribed. There is a universal inclusiveness in it.

Let us now turn to consider that other genealogy found in Luke. Luke's genealogy, unlike that of Matthew as we have seen, is traced backwards, beginning with Jesus making use particularly of the genealogy we first mentioned, Genesis 5:3-32. Luke's genealogy is longer than that of Matthew containing 77 names, and especially in the near 1,000-year period between David and Jesus Luke's 42 generations fit far better than Matthew's mere 28. Matthew uses his 42 generations to go unrealistically not from David to Jesus but rather from Abraham to Jesus. Again, we could be in the realm of numerology for it is immediately clear that both numbers are multiples of seven. Seven is a holy number while twelve is understood as the true number of God's people, hence the twelve tribes of Israel, the twelve apostles and the numbers worshipping God in the heavens (Revelation 7:1-8). Further to numerology we possibly have here in Luke's account seven times eleven giving the 77 names with Jesus representing completion making the perfect twelve or maybe twelve by seven giving 84 which when divided by two gives the 42 generations between David as king and this new king of David's line. Again, this can only of course be conjecture but the numbers seem to have intentionality about them.

As noted above Luke rather than placing the genealogy at the beginning of the gospel with Jesus' birth, as in the case of Matthew, places it at the beginning of Jesus' ministry, immediately following his telling us of the ministry of John the Baptist (3:23-38). In doing this he seems to be intentionally paralleling the likewise placement of Moses' genealogy after his being summoned, and just before the commencement of his ministry (Exodus 6:16-25). As such again we find the Mosaic concern of which I have spoken is not limited to Matthew's gospel.

Crucially the placement of this section of Luke's Gospel, before the story of Jesus' ministry begins, may indicate something crucial to our whole topic, that this genealogy lay at the beginning of a proto-Lukan gospel before the nativity story was later inserted into it. Given that many scholars now believe that Luke's gospel may have been composed as late as the early second century this would serve as further evidence that the whole infancy narrative tradition is one which developed very late, perhaps being only present in Matthew until it made an appearance in another form in Luke as the final layer of tradition in the gospel, maybe more than a century after the events it describes! There is however no textual evidence for this assertion.

As noted earlier Luke traces his genealogy right back to Adam, this often being understood as a sign of his universal concern, something which carries right through his gospel. Thus, he calls Adam 'son of God' (Luke 3:38) in the conclusion of his genealogy. Current Jewish speculation saw Adam as 'son of God' being a heavenly figure. With Jesus, already being named 'son of God' in his baptism, that account being placed by Luke immediately prior to this genealogy, Luke appears to be saying a new humanity is being founded in Jesus given the link to the one, Adam, the first 'son of God,' in whom humanity had its genesis. Like Adam perhaps Jesus is also being viewed as a heavenly figure but in his case already being so during his lifetime, the heavens after all having just opened in his baptism. In any case by the time he is writing Luke clearly regards Jesus as such a heavenly figure in whom is founded a new humanity/creation.

This universal concern means Luke prefers to call Jesus by this title, 'son of God,' a title well known in much of the ancient world, in contrast to Matthew who gives Jesus the more exclusivist Jewish nationalist term, 'Messiah.' This term 'son of God' was commonly ascribed to great rulers in the ancient world such as Alexander the Great and the Caesars of Rome so Luke by his co-option of such a term is affirming that in

Jesus one is present who, like those figures, is ruler among rulers. It is an audacious claim of course as Jesus, disgracefully executed by the empire, clearly lacked any of the power attributes normally associated with 'son of God' figures. Luke contends however that this ruler among rulers comes from a radically different place and in so doing turns the concepts of rule and power on their head. Already in the Magnificat he has spoken of how in the annunciation of the birth of Jesus, '[God] has shown the power of his arm, routed the proud of heart, pulled the princes from their thrones and exalted the lowly, the hungry he has filled with good things, and the rich he has sent empty away' (Luke 1:46-55). Luke in thus radically re-orienting 'rule' and 'power' is able then to affirm that Jesus, the one executing these things, though in a very different form, can therefore rightly be called, 'son of God.'

Luke, as we have seen, also has an interest in emphasising Jesus' priestly line in his genealogy and so in his list of names following the exile frequently uses names like Levi and Mattathias thereby implying Jesus' descent through the priestly house of Levi. In like manner he presents Elizabeth, the mother of John the Baptist, as coming from Levitical descent (Luke 1:5). Given that Mary is Elizabeth's kinswoman it would seem to be implied that Jesus has Levitical descent on his mother's side. That contrast between Matthew who emphasises the royal line of Jesus through David and Luke who emphasises the priestly line was noted as long ago c. 220 CE by Julius Africanus. Thus, it could be broadly said that Matthew is emphasising Jesus as king while Luke is emphasising Jesus as priest. Once again, we may remind ourselves of the Dead Sea tradition which understood the coming Messiah to be both king of the Davidic line and priest from the line of Aaron but understood the latter being of far greater importance.

Far from being a boring or meaningless part of our two gospels, to be quickly passed over, the genealogies tell us much about how both Matthew and Luke understand Jesus. Both have their emphases as we have seen, though not to the total exclusion of the other. Thus, while Matthew emphasises the Mosaic and Davidic roots of Jesus as the Messiah come to inaugurate a new Israel that more universal concern normally associated with Luke is not missing from his gospel as we have

3: The Family Tree

seen for Jesus comes out of the line of Abraham the one in whom is not only founded a new Israel but a new humanity. In both the genealogies constructed by Matthew and Luke of Jesus we find the central idea of Jesus as a new genesis, not only of Israel but of humanity itself. He is both king and priest bringing together the two strands of the Messianic tradition, the Davidic and the Aaronic, and is even announced as being 'son of God', one who would present a direct challenge to those rulers of the ancient world bearing that nomenclature.

There is of course an immediate problem in constructing a genealogy for Jesus, that clearly being the developing virgin birth tradition found in these two same gospels in which we have the genealogies. Genealogies of course were drawn through the male line but how can Jesus be 'begat' by Joseph when we are already being told that his birth was miraculous with no male input save that of the Divine? This is further complicated in that in antiquity male input into the birth was the only thing that counted as it was believed the mother biologically was nothing more than a receptacle within which the male seed developed, with her contributing nothing more to the off-spring. [3] Given their use of the virgin birth both Matthew and Luke must make clear in their genealogies that Joseph is not the real father. So, difficult is this task for Matthew that in concluding the lineage he, after a pattern of 'so and so begot so and so and so begot so and so' concludes irregularly with 'Jacob begot Joseph to whom was betrothed Mary the mother of Jesus' (Matthew 1:16). This represents the main line of the textual tradition. What I mean by saying this is that we need to recognise that with none of the gospels, nor indeed the Scriptures as a whole, do we have a single unified text but rather one constructed by scholars weighing the merits of the many different textual variants. [4] Thus, in this section of Matthew's gospel as in almost all other places there are other textual traditions. That there are so many variant traditions in this place shows just how difficult it was for those in the early church to deal with this conundrum of Jesus, like all great men, needing a genealogy traced through the paternal line yet having his mother being a virgin. One of these variants, the Ebionite tradition, which rejected the virgin birth has, 'Jacob begot Joseph, to whom was betrothed Mary the virgin, begot

Jesus.' Here by a clever use of syntax it is seemingly being argued that just as Jacob begot Joseph so did Joseph, betrothed to a virgin, beget Jesus. The note that Joseph was betrothed to Mary the virgin is merely given in passing almost in brackets and in so bracketed results in the usual lineage being apparently given through the father. Luke solves the problem by claiming that Joseph was merely the putative father of Jesus, 'Jesus being the son, as was supposed, of Joseph' (Luke 3:23). In conclusion, we should note that the Gospel of John has no problem with Joseph being Jesus' father, it being simply assumed (John 6:42). There the crowd reject Jesus precisely because of their familiarity with his ordinariness, being, 'the son of Joseph.' Despite the understanding of the earliest layer of tradition prior to Matthew and Luke, and that of John, that Jesus' birth was quite natural, it was the miraculous birth tradition which would win out in the developing Christian tradition.

It is to that miraculous birth to which we now turn.

Endnotes

1 The Babylonian exile represented a great crisis of faith for the Jewish people a total catastrophe for a people who defined themselves by their being freed from slavery in Egypt by a liberating God. Of course, when we speak of the Babylonian exile we are speaking only of the southern kingdom of Judah as the northern tribes had been taken into slavery by the Assyrians some 150 years earlier and they then simply disappear from history. Judah viewed their survival from Assyrian captivity as miraculous being a powerful affirmation that God was with them and would always even miraculously protect them. Hence the total crisis of identity with the Babylonian captivity. One of the ways in which they dealt with this crisis was by postulating that one day they would be ruled by a Messiah and with the coming of that Messiah all other nations would stream to them and they, rather than being ruled, would rule the nations.

2 Given the central role that David is to play in this gospel being the figure after whom Jesus was based, it seems that Matthew (1:6) given his high regard for David can't bring himself to actually name the woman with whom David so shamefully acted. The account of David's adulterous liaison with Bathsheba may be found in 2 Samuel 11.

3 With the discovery of the mother's input into the child beyond being a mere receptacle for the male seed in the 19th century some saw it as necessary to preserve Jesus' mother, Mary from the stain from sexual procreation which she would have of course passed on to him. The response of the Roman Catholic Church was to promulgate in 1854 the doctrine of the Immaculate Conception whereby Mary had been born miraculously free from sexual input. Thus, now both Jesus' father and mother were free from the taint of sexual input.

4 There is no one text of the Scriptures which comes to us as the 'correct' text. The earliest full text we have for the Christian Scriptures comes from the 4th century while that for the

3: The Family Tree

Hebrew Scriptures only went back to the 10th century until the discovery of the Dead Sea Scrolls in 1947 which showed how fastidious the scribes had been in carrying out their task accurately. Instead of relying on those late full texts scholars must sift through the thousands of manuscript scraps which have been found with there often being numerous variant texts on the one passage. They then must determine which variant has the most support. This not as easy as it sounds. The factors used in their determination are the date of the text, this being not so much the age of the manuscript but rather the date of the tradition from which it comes (and in that we are already in danger of the circular argument), the breadth of the geographical distribution, the nature of the grammar with simpler grammar usually being seen as coming later as a clean-up, the length of the variant, the shorter being usually preferred unless it comes from an ellipse (a copyist's eye jumping a line) and if the longer has something added which is clearly a pious addition ('Jesus went to the temple' is preferred to 'Jesus, the son of God, went to the temple'), and last the more scandalous or unorthodox reading is probably right as it would have been later 'corrected.' The consensus gives us what is called the 'received text.' The strength of the received text will be marked with an A, B, C, or D, A being the strongest attestation that the text used is the correct one and D meaning it is the most contested. In most English translations only, those in the category D will be noted. Nearly all variants are assigned an A or a B but there are some significant passages given a C or D. Thus, a C is assigned to John 20:31, a crucial passage determining the purpose for the writing of the gospel. There are strong textual variants for the reading, 'that you may continue to believe' but also for 'that you may come to believe.' Is the gospel one meant to strengthen those already believing or is its purpose evangelistic, to bring others to believe? The latter has the strongest evidence, but it is contestable. One Greek letter in this case, an iota (i) makes all the difference.

4: Virgin Mother!

Of all stumbling blocks to belief in the Christmas stories the idea of the virgin birth is perhaps the strongest, for the idea of a woman being both virgin and mother naturally strikes us as total impossibility. Yet both our nativity stories claim this of Jesus' birth from Mary. Further as the tradition developed this virgin birth tradition was further strengthened in that it came to be claimed that not only was Mary virgin at the time of Jesus birth but that she maintained a perpetual virginity, this despite Jesus even having siblings named in the gospels.

Again, we are dealing only with the two gospel accounts given in Matthew and Luke when we speak of the virgin birth with the earlier layers of the tradition in Paul and Mark, nor the Johannine tradition, knowing anything of it, while segments of the church, the Ebionites, as we have seen, Cerinthus (c.100 CE) and Marcion (c.160 CE), along with the Gnostics, among others, continued to reject it even after it had entered the tradition.

There have been some attempts to find hints of the virgin birth in earlier traditions in the Scriptures making use of such passages as those written by Paul as Galatians 4:4 where he states, 'God sent forth his son, born of a woman,' with no mention of paternity, and Romans 1:3 where Jesus is understood as being descended from David, 'according to the flesh' as though the real descent lay elsewhere. Again, likewise it is claimed that the virgin birth is hinted in Mark when Jesus is called the 'son of Mary and brother of James, Joses, Judas and Simon' with his unnamed sisters then mentioned but no father given (Mark 6:3). Most likely here of course there is no reference to the father due to an entirely natural reason of his being deceased. I can only surmise that on each of the above occasions a long-bow is being drawn to find evidence, by reading into the text, from what clearly is an already pre-determined position.

It is most likely that the virgin birth doesn't enter the tradition until Matthew introduces it some 80-85 years after the event. Even after that however one of our gospels, John seemingly knows nothing of it, or if knowing does not feel a need to use it. Though he writes, 'he who was begotten not of humanity, nor will of the flesh, not of human will but that of God (John 1:13) it is again a huge stretch to claim here that John is indicating a belief in the virgin birth especially so when we find later in the very same chapter that John sees no conflict in claiming that Jesus is both 'the son of Joseph' and yet also 'the son of God' (John 1:45 c.f. 49). For John clearly having a human father does not preclude Jesus being one born of God. Paul likewise concurs with this writing, 'for as many as led by the Spirit of God they are the children of God' (Romans 8:9-17). It is unlikely that Paul believed all these being led by the Spirit had been born or re-born in a miraculous manner of God! Rather their physical births were understood to be entirely natural. Being born of such natural means clearly does not for Paul and John exclude one from being a 'child of God.'

Elsewhere in the apocryphal gospels and the early tradition the virgin birth is found in the opening chapter of the Gospel of the Hebrews and in the writings of Ignatius of Antioch (c.35-50 to 98-110 CE) (Letter to the Ephesians 7:2, 18:2a, 19:1 and Letter to the Smyrnaeans 1: 1-2). We would expect such as all these are representative of the developing virgin birth tradition.

By the second century the idea of the virgin birth was becoming Christian orthodoxy with the nature of it, like all miraculous stories, becoming ever more stupendous, an example being in the second century gospel, the Protovangelium of James, where Mary is described as giving birth miraculously with her sexual organs still intact. The ever more miraculous nature of the birth would culminate of course in the Roman Catholic and Orthodox Church doctrine of the perpetual virginity of Mary. By such Mary was virgin before birth (ante partum) in birth (in partu, often implying that the hymen was unbroken) and after birth (post-partum asserting that she never had any sexual relationship with Joseph). Jesus' siblings are said to either be cousins or are from a previous marriage of Joseph. Thus, by the time of the writing of the First Apocalypse of James, found among the Nag Hammadi library and probably dating to 180-250 CE, James, the most famous of Jesus' brothers, has already become a half-brother. As already charged, only

4: Virgin Mother!

in doggedly defending an already determined position would we find such clear words in the Scriptures themselves that Jesus had siblings to be made into meaning something else! Those who from a Protestant position reject the idea that Mary was perpetually virgin will be no doubt surprised to learn that this doctrine was accepted by the 16th century Protestant Reformers though of course it is held by few Protestants today.

Again, in those gospels central to our discussion, Matthew and Luke when we come to the virgin birth we, as with other parts of the Christmas story, tend to conflate our two gospels but it should be noted that the virgin birth claim is overwhelmingly one made from Matthew with evidence for it not particularly strong in Luke's gospel with it being hinted only in two verses (Luke 1:34, 3:23). Otherwise the birth in Luke appears normal with Joseph consistently being referred to as the father. This would make the birth consistent with how the writers of the Hebrew Scriptures understood God acting in the births of anyone understood to have something miraculous about their birth as we shall see. Miraculous though those births may be they were all by natural means, a result of sexual intercourse. The virgin birth represents something radically new in the biblical tradition!

The opponents of Jesus had no time for supernatural explanations of his birth instead holding that the whole thing concerning Jesus' virgin birth had been concocted by the Christians in order to hide the shame of their master's questionable paternity. Echoes of that polemic may even be seen in the gospels in such passages where those opposing Jesus make much of their father being Abraham implicitly thereby questioning Jesus' paternity (Matthew 3:9, Luke 3:8, John 8: 33, 39) and more explicitly where John has them in the same encounter charge, 'we were not born of fornication; we have one father, even God' (John 8:41). Such words are hardly what one would class as a subtle dig made at the expense of Jesus' questionable paternity! Again, due to the embarrassment factor seemingly these charges were so well known that even though they may cause discomfiture to the gospel writers they cannot expunge them from their writings. That there was strong questioning of Jesus' paternity seemingly dating back to his own lifetime seems very well established.

It is easy for us to forget the shame associated with being born or even conceived out of wedlock. Those of us who are older will still remember the social shame of a child thus born or even a woman 'falling pregnant' while unmarried. The result of the latter was that many were born 'premature' seven or eight months after a hastily concluded marriage. I remember quite clearly, though I was too young to really understand, an older pregnant but un-wed cousin been spirited away mysteriously up country in an attempt to avoid familial shame. It is not that long ago that there were also legal ramifications to do with inheritance for being born a 'bastard,' that word having a technical definition, born from an un-wed couple. So removed have we become of course from such attitudes that many using that word today would scarcely understand its specific meaning!

The scandal associated with Jesus' birth would lead to the later charge made by opponents, mainly Jewish, of the Christian faith that Jesus was the off-spring of a liaison between Mary and a Roman soldier, Pantera or Panthera. We find this charge, referred to by Origen, in the works of Celsus (c.178) (Contra Celsus, Origen, 1:28), and in the Jewish Talmud (Jebamoth/Yebamoth: 49A, Babylonian Shabbath, 104 b, repeated in almost identical words in the Babylonian Sanhedrin, 67 a). Even as late as the 4th century St Epiphanius, the Bishop of Salamis (315-403) again confirmed the ben Panthera story, this champion of Christian orthodoxy and saint of Roman Catholicism frankly stating, 'Jesus was the son of a certain Julius whose surname was Panthera.' (Heresies, Epip., Haer, Epiphanius, lxxvii, 7.) That a bishop could hold such a view so late shows just how marginal the nativity narrative was to the early church!

Indeed, the growth of this polemic around Jesus' questionable legitimacy is probably largely instrumental for the virgin birth story entering the developing Christian tradition as a means of defence from such charges, some 85-90 years as we have seen, after the events described. Earlier across the range of opinion concerning Jesus there seemingly was an acceptance of the normality of his birth and it seems only when the Jewish polemic concerning his dubious birth, grew sufficiently strong do we get the development of the virgin birth tradition. The growing antipathy, of which I have spoken, between

4: Virgin Mother!

those who from the Jewish tradition followed Jesus, the Jesus Jews, and those who from that same Jewish background rejected Jesus meant that the latter of course began understandably to make increasing use of the entirely natural question as to the legitimacy of paternity of Jesus in their polemic. How could, they charged, one of illegitimate birth be the Messiah? Seemingly lacking an effective means of defence by reference to Joseph as Jesus' father, for as we have seen doubts to his paternity go way back, the response increasingly of the Church was the virgin birth story. Thus so could Jesus' legitimacy as Messiah be defended. Further the defence seemed to carry within it an extra bonus as by it the Church could not only defend their saviour against the charges being bought concerning his birth but by such special birth narrative also succeed in raising one of very humble and even scandalous birth to the ranks of the kings and gods.

The assertion that Mary gave birth miraculously as a virgin actually arises from a mistaken translation from the Hebrew to the Greek. In developing the virgin birth defence, Matthew the gospel writer, as noted most strongly identified with it, makes a crucial error in that passage he quotes from the Hebrew Scriptures in order to seal his case.

To the modern scholar Scripture speaks of course in an historical manner only to that past event to which it refers but for the believer at that time it stood a-historically, the veracity of the current event shown in how it stood in line of past Scriptural events, with those past things often seen as even prophesying or predicting it. This is somewhat analogous to how a modern fundamentalist uses Scripture. For such a believer, something in the Scriptures clearly referring to an event of the time in which it was written becomes a thing which is making a contemporary statement. Thus, the beast of the Book of Revelation becomes a-historically linked with modern empires as though in reality it was speaking of them when of course its reference is limited to that empire centred on Rome even if there it need be cryptically called 'Babylon.'

As we have seen both Matthew and Luke have made use of past Scripture in this manner to both describe and prove contemporary events in their renditions of the Christmas story and Matthew again does so when it comes to the virgin birth. This was something very commonly done in the Jewish tradition and it is known as midrash. This hermeneutical practice involved the recital of Scriptural and other stories to bring out their religious import in a contemporary setting by using an imaginative interpretation or expansion of the older text. The method particularly enabled the writer to establish the veracity of the divine presence being in a current event or person by linking it to an occasion in the divine tradition, where it was universally held that the divine had indeed been present. The Christmas stories are filled with examples of midrash and parallels as we shall further explore. Suffice to give some examples now from the nativity story; Matthew 1:23 (the virgin birth) being drawn, as we have seen, from Isaiah 7:14, Matthew 2:15 (concerning Jesus remaining in Egypt) from Hosea 11:1 and Matthew 2:17-18 (a voice crying in Ramah following the massacre of the innocents) from Jeremiah 31:15. This is all easy to see as any reputable bible translation will show these parallels in the footnotes at each page.

Before continuing to better understand midrash as an excursus let us look at an example of this use central to the biblical story; being able to miraculously able to control water. As we probably know Moses in the parting of the Red Sea (Exodus 14) was the first to do something miraculous with water and in that action God was seen to be present for only God had the ability to control the waters, as seen in the creation story where the divine is able to bring order out of chaos by controlling the primeval waters (Genesis 1: 6-10). Of course, Moses, being judged by his lack of faith while in the desert at Massah and Meribah, where there is another water miracle (Exodus 17: 1-7), is only permitted to see the 'Promised Land' from Mount Nebo but not enter it. That entry will take place under his successor Joshua with any question of his legitimacy as a successor of Moses being dealt with by he, like Moses, having that ability to likewise part water, in his case the Jordan River enabling the 'children of Israel' to enter the land (Joshua 3). Later in the sacred tradition the greatest of the prophets, Elijah is shown to have this ability to divide water (2 Kings 2:7-8), an ability which as seen shows God is present with him. Following his being taken in a fiery chariot into heaven his mantle is passed to Elisha with the legitimacy of that succession being established in that Elisha like Elijah had the ability to part waters, that parting proving the divine being with him also (2 Kings 2:13-14). When we come to Jesus the gospel writers trump all of this in having Jesus, unlike those before him, without reference to God but just in his own powers, do even greater things with water than them. Thus, he stills it (Mark 4:35-41) and even walks upon it (Mark 6:45-52). As such this is all classic midrash.

Let us now return to the virgin birth story. As we have already noted the Gospel writers usually when they quote from the Jewish Scriptures make use of a Greek translation the Septuagint or LXX which as we have seen had been written with the needs of the diaspora of the Jews to all parts of the Greek and then later Roman Empire in mind. The problem of course as anyone with bi-lingual skills will know is that sometimes translation from one language to another is not as straight-forward as we would like to think. Concepts in one language are often difficult to capture in another and sometimes a less appropriate word is used in the language into which the translation is being made than should be the case. While mostly a translation represents a genuine attempt at correctly translating, words in different languages accumulate all manner of nuances. Thus, to translate the Spanish 'popular' into English as popular would be to ignore the different meanings accumulating around the word in each language (the Spanish has a more sociological 'folk' tradition around it than the English where it is more linked to the mere numbers, often understood pejoratively, attached to a thing which makes it popular). Often the mistake is not intentional but of course sometimes the mistranslation can be very deliberate. An example is the Maori and English words around the idea of 'sovereignty' in the founding document of New Zealand, the 'Treaty of Waitangi,' meaning something quite different. A more accurate translation would have almost certainly caused the Maori not to assent to the treaty. As to the deliberate nature or otherwise of this and of the Matthean mistranslation of the passage from Isaiah we can never entirely of course know.

In the Matthean virgin birth narrative the inaccuracy of translation, intentional or otherwise, comes when Matthew speaks of how 'a virgin shall conceive and bear a son' (Matthew 1:23). This mistranslation comes about because Matthew is using the Greek Septuagint which incorrectly had translated the Hebrew of Isaiah 7:14 specifically as 'virgin' when it more generally means 'young woman.' We cannot really know whether Matthew makes this mistranslation because he doesn't have sufficient knowledge of Hebrew or that having sufficient knowledge of Hebrew he is deliberately covering up, or perhaps neither of these, but rather that having become accustomed to using the LXX translation he does so again here without further thought as to what the Hebrew actually said. While it is impossible to know as to Matthew's intentionality or otherwise here, and I suspect there is some intentionality, in any case on this occasion the LXX mistranslation dovetails very nicely with Matthew's theology, coincidence or otherwise. The mistake is very clear and was pointed out quickly by opponents of the virgin birth tradition and was owned up to in the Christian tradition as early as the second century by Justin Martyr (c.100-c.165CE) (Dialogue with Tyyho: 84).

The passage in question, Isaiah 7:14, from where Matthew draws his 'proof,' in its original context, as composed by Isaiah, is a promise made in a time of crisis to Ahaz, an 8th century BCE king of Judah, as to how his Judean lineage would continue despite all the threats of impending doom to the land of Judah from the surrounding Assyrian army, specifically the armies of Syria, and the northern kingdom of Israel, two nations allied to that superpower. Amid this seemingly hopeless situation the prophet Isaiah speaks declaring, 'Therefore the Lord himself will give you a sign. Behold the young woman with child will soon give birth to a son and shall call him Immanuel....before the child knows how to refuse evil and choose the good, the land before whose two kings you are in dread, will be deserted' (Isaiah 7: 14, 16) before adding, 'be broken you peoples and be dismayed; give ear all you far countries; gird yourselves and be dismayed....take counsel together, but it will come to naught (Isaiah 8:9-10).' The giving of the name, Immanuel, 'God is with us' was especially propitious in that context of war. No attempt is made however to suggest that the prince to be born; Hezekiah, will be born by any other than the usual means. Neither is there any messianic use made in the Jewish tradition of this passage. Further the prophecy in Isaiah speaks of a woman already with child rather than one still without child yet to

4: Virgin Mother!

conceive, this inconsistency being very early on pointed out by Jewish opponents of such use of the Isaiah passage. While there was a wide expectation of a coming Messiah within Judaism it was never expected that the birth of such a figure would take place in any but the normal means. Matthew of course is happy to make a-historical use of such a passage especially when it was mistranslated in the Greek Septuagint version. Ben Witherington tellingly concludes there is, 'no evidence that any early Jew saw this as a prophecy about the Messiah, much less a prophecy about virginal conception.' [1]

Interestingly after being used just the one time in the infancy narratives so to prove the veracity of Jesus' birth, this highly appropriate title for Jesus, 'Immanuel,' is never used again, even though Matthew in his nativity account informs us that is what he will indeed be called (Matthew 1:23)! Again, this difference between the main body of the gospel and the nativity story indicates, as we have already seen with Luke's gospel, that the nativity story in Matthew is probably a distinct late part of the tradition in the construction of this gospel.

The Hebrew word originally used by Isaiah 'almah should best be translated 'young woman' and not as 'virgin' for Hebrew reserves another word, betulah more specifically for that designation. In the Hebrew Scriptures 'almah refers to a sexually mature young woman, one who has passed through puberty who may or may not be a virgin. However, even that word, betulah in Hebrew more specifically used of virgin has an elasticity about it in that it could also mean 'bodily immaturity' and thus the inability to conceive rather than being strictly about virginity per se. This is an important distinction in a society where very early marriage and therefore sexual activity was prevalent so that it was quite possible that a girl could lose her virginity before the advent of her menstrual cycle. Indeed, some like Rabbi Eliezer ben Hyrcanus about 70 years after the time of Jesus believed that a woman remained a virgin after sexual intercourse and even after childbirth if she had not yet commenced menstruation (Mishnah Niddah 1:4, 6). That linking of virginity with the menstrual cycle meant strangely enough even a post-menopausal woman could once again regain a virginal status. Thus, the famous Jewish philosopher Philo of Alexandria, a near contemporary of Jesus, when speaking of Sarah, wife of Abraham, claims of her post-menopausal that she is a virgin for the second time (De posteritate Caini 134) with her offspring Isaac being named by him, given his miraculous conception through a 'virgin,' 'son of God' (De Mutatione Nominum 131, De Cherubim 45).

From the rabbinic age shortly following the time of Jesus we have evidence that pre-pubescent marriage was generally permitted with majority being considered to have been reached when one turned 12 years. Such was the early age of marriage that rabbinic practice included the arguing of whether blood stains on the sheets of the nuptial bed were the markings of a first period or those resulting from the breaking of the hymen in the consummation of the marriage. Given this young age of marriage it was quite possible for a young woman to conceive prior to her first menstrual period and still be considered a virgin.

The mistaken translation in the Septuagint, which had resulted in the incorrect Matthean lifting of the passage in question to argue the virgin birth, was rectified in later translations of that document in the 1st and 2nd centuries CE with the Greek term neanis meaning young woman being substituted for parthenos. Parthenos specifically means 'one put aside' understood usually as being a virgin and when ordinarily used in the Septuagint it renders the Hebrew 'betulah or naara where virginity was more clearly meant by the Hebrew authors. This distinction may be seen in Genesis 24 where in verse 16 the former, 'betulah is translated in English as 'virgin' while a little later, in verse 43 'almah is translated 'young woman' with the status as to virginity left unspecified. In using the word parthenos rather than neanis Matthew avoided the ambiguity of the latter word which could be used as a translation of numerous Hebrew terms words meaning 'virgin', 'girl' and 'young woman.' His intention is thus apparently clear when he uses this word, a desire to make clear that Jesus was born of a virgin. Yet the matter is further complicated when we realise that the Greek parthenos itself, like the Hebrew betulah primarily denoted age rather than the marital status of a person. Thus, a person could be married and still be considered a virgin, even after intercourse, if they had not come of age, this being tied, as we have seen with the Hebrew understanding, to menstruation. Within the Septuagint parthenos is used more widely to signify a girl who was young or unmarried with all three Hebrew terms 'almah, 'betulah or naara being on occasions translated as parthenos. The result is that we have numerous tombstones attesting to parthenoi or 'married virgins.' This is all very confusing and shows just how imprecise language can be on occasions, even more so when translation is involved. In any case it is a step too far to take the Hebrew 'almah and make of it something as definitive as virgin as we understand that word in English.

Given that the intention of the original author, Isaiah, was clear in that he was speaking not of a virgin but simply of a young woman, indeed one already with child, the best translation into Greek in the Septuagint would have been the less specific 'neanis' rather than parthenos. In any case as we have seen even both the Hebrew 'betulah and Greek parthenos, words more specifically indicating virginity, still have a great deal of elasticity in them. As Geza Vermes writes, 'the only conclusion one needs to draw from all this is that virginity and virgin birth were much more elastic notions in Jewish antiquity than Christian tradition allows.' [2] In light of this, we can conclude that the virgin birth is much more complex and becomes progressively less and less miraculous than it is at first reading.

In the Hebrew tradition pre-matrimonial virginity was highly prized (Genesis 24:1b, Leviticus 21: 13-14, Esther 2:2) with chastity being assumed of all reputable unmarried young women (Deuteronomy 22:21), this seemingly being maintained (Judges 21:12) except in situations of dire straits (Judges 19:24). [3] Virgins were guarded (2 Samuel 13:2) and violation brought shame (2 Samuel 13:12-13, Deuteronomy 22:14). Indeed, an absence of virginity before marriage could even lead to a woman being stoned (Deuteronomy 22:21), the result being that any false accusation was also taken very seriously (Deuteronomy 22:18-19). In the event of rape, it was held that marriage must follow (Deuteronomy 22: 28-29), except when the woman refuses the man in which case a bride price must still be paid (Exodus 22:16-17). Finally, fornication with an engaged virgin was understood as adultery and required the death penalty (Deuteronomy 22: 23-27). Of course, it is difficult to know how strenuously these laws were enforced.

In any case, given the above, we can see just how precarious was the position of Mary. As presented in both gospels the birth of Jesus takes place with Mary and Joseph betrothed to each other. Betrothal was legally binding with the couple cohabiting together, thus Joseph's perceived need to leave rather than publicly divorce her. For him not to do so quietly may have, as we have noted, lead even to the death penalty being invoked against Mary for her supposed infidelity. Thus, we are told he, being, 'a man of honour' intended to do 'the honourable thing' and leave quietly before receiving revelation in a dream that he should remain for Mary was pregnant by means of the Holy Spirit (Matthew 1:19-20). That Matthew wishes to emphasise that Mary conceives as a virgin is seen in his conclusion to this episode where he emphatically states that Joseph did not have intercourse with Mary before the birth (Matthew 1:25). How he could know that of course we cannot know. It almost appears that he must have been keeping watch in the bedroom some 85 years beforehand!

The understanding of the virgin birth, as I have noted, continued to develop following the Scriptural period with the belief that Mary was virgin at the time of Jesus' birth, soon developing into that of her being perpetually virgin. There is of course a problem, as we have seen, with this idea for we are clearly told in the Scriptures, from two different traditions, that Jesus had brothers, James, Joseph, Simon and Judas as well as unnamed sisters (Mark 6: 3, Matthew 13:55-56). Further Luke tells us that Jesus is Mary's 'first born' implying that she had more (Luke 2:7), the word used prototokos indicating that, whereas the word which would be better used specifically to indicate 'only born' would be one clearly indicating such, 'monogenes.'

Given the uncleanliness associated with the acct of childbirth in both the Jewish and Christian traditions, (something we will examine later) this development of the perpetual virginity of Mary is understandable in that it removed sex from the procreation of Jesus. That made special sense in the developing Christian tradition which finally became obsessive about sex to the point of being what can only be called, neurotic. Both the doctrine of the perpetual virginity of Mary and the Christian aversion to sex grow together.

4: Virgin Mother!

That process of removing Mary, and therefore Jesus, from any dint of sexual activity continued finally culminating in the 19th century doctrine of the Immaculate Conception (1854). The specific reason for the promulgation of this doctrine was probably, as already noted, the biological discovery that a woman had input into the seed of the child, being much more than what was thought up until then, a mere receptacle of the man's growing seed. We still talk in such manner when we speak of horses saying that a foal was 'sired' out of a mare as though only the stallion had input into the foal. The discovery of the female biological input into the child meant of course that the 'ugly stain' of sex through Mary herself having been conceived through a sexual act, would necessarily still be associated with the birth of Jesus. The father may well have been God meaning no male sexual input was involved but the mother was one born out of a carnal sexual act, and given that now it was understood that the mother passed what we know as genes into her progeny it became necessary to have her, like the 'father', removed from a sexual act, such being understood as something inherently evil by which a stain known as original sin was passed on to each generation from the one before it. By the Immaculate Conception Mary could be taken out of that stained genetic lineage, the result being that Jesus could have purity of input both paternally and maternally.

Of course, in constructing the divine/human virgin birth stories the gospel writers don't draw those stories out of nowhere. Births outside of natural biological means, usually involving gods, had a long and wide pedigree in the ancient world, with that pedigree extending not only to the pagan but also to the Jewish tradition, though in the latter the miraculous never included anything outside of normal coitus between two human beings.

Of this wide dispersal, and therefore proof of the power of the myth of births involving divine-human liaisons, a few examples will suffice. The most interesting of these is the myth of Nana the mother of Attis, known successively in different cultural traditions under other names as Inanna, Osiris, Dionysius, Tammuz and Orpheus, all figures linked to virginal conception. Nana as a virgin conceives Attis, whom we may note was later crucified upon a pine tree, his followers then eating his body while his blood was spilled to renew the earth. After three days he returned to life! The similarities to the Christian story are such that they hardly need to be pointed out.

Elsewhere, Zeus impregnates Alkeme while taking the form of Anphitryon, her husband, leading to the birth of Herakles (Hercules). Herakles elevated to be a god then in turn with the mortal Auge, daughter of King Aleus of Tegea, fathers Telephus. Again, likewise Perseus is born of a union between Zeus and Danae. Alexander the Great was believed to have been born of a union between Zeus (again!) and the mortal Olympias. That Philip, the supposed father of Alexander, receives this vision in a dream will again sound familiar to us. In the various accounts of the birth of Romulus, founder of Rome, he was sometimes seen to be the issue of a union between a god and a human. One of the birth myths associated with him has him being the offspring of Mars and Aemilia, while in another version of the Roman origin story Tarchetius has a revelatory dream (again sound familiar!) that his daughter will bear a mighty son. When the daughter refuses the god and instead sends her maidservant who is impregnated, Tachetius orders Romulus and Remus killed at birth. Hidden by a river bank and later found (think Moses), after being suckled by a wolf, they survive. The Moses story is again paralleled in the tradition of the country in which it of course had taken place; Egypt. There the god Horus, while still a child, is hidden by his mother Isis by being placed in a reed boat in a papyrus marshland. From Mesopotamia the Akkadians likewise had a story where Sargon, the mighty king was placed by his mother, a high priestess, in a basket of rushes before sealing the lid with bitumen. The philosopher Plato by some accounts was also believed to be born without paternity. The parallels come jumping out at us! To show the traffic was not entirely all one way; male gods to female mortals, the goddess Aphrodite bears Aeneas from the seed of a human father, Anchises. We need note however, and I shall return to this, that such miraculous divine births are all associated with significant people.

We may note that in far-away India Queen Mayadevi dreams of a white elephant descending from a heaven entering her right side leading to the conception of a child who would later be known as the Buddha.

4: Virgin Mother!

That the divine/human birth myth was so widely dispersed clearly indicates just how profoundly deeply it ran within the ancient world, it seeming to come out of some deep human need whereby it seemed only appropriate for great men, and they were always men, to have divine input into their births with those births then being often associated with other miraculous portents.

Many of course in defending the Christian story are quick to argue that these pagan divine-human liaisons are crudely sexual in comparison with the asexual generation found in the Christian infancy narratives wherein it is asserted the Holy Spirit doesn't operate in like crude manner as a male agent impregnating the mother, but rather as a creative force overshadowing her. (This idea of the Holy Spirit overshadowing Mary has links to the Hebrew understanding of the shekinah, the divine presence upon earth, this concept having been developed as a means of excluding any anthropomorphism concerning the earthy divine presence). As to the supposed crudity of the pagan stories in comparison with the biblical story many such arguments are far too simplistic, for on looking at the pagan stories we find many are not crudely sexual but rather often have that same deeply symbolic understanding of the divine/human procreative act in like manner to the gospels. Thus, the Greek writer Plutarch speaks of the Egyptian belief of divine generation being through the 'power' or 'spirit' of God, this being like the Jewish 'shekinah.' Of course, fuelling much of this attempt to distinguish the Christian story from other supposedly crudely sexual narratives of the pagan world is the aversion of the Church to sex and sexuality.

Further it is often argued that such a strong pagan influence would not have been acceptable to the early Christians, still so much under the influence of Judaism. As to this objection we have already seen how these same Christian writers often make use of the pagan tradition, and we will find as we move on further such connections. This is only to be expected for one after-all is not, because of their specific religious conviction, isolated from wider cultural influences. Judaism itself was shot through with these influences with the vigorous protest of some Jews to pagan influence clearly proving the point for one hardly protests something which is non-existent!

A recurring theme in many of the pagan stories of antiquity is that those born of divine/human liaisons by their heroic actions gain access to heaven. It soon likewise became the Christian belief that Jesus by his heroic actions on the cross won, not only for himself but for his followers as well, the heavenly realm with Paul particularly speaking very much in such manner (Colossians 1:13). Having this heroic role Jesus then needs like status in his birth to these other heroes.

Miraculous birth stories however are not only seen in the pagan writings of the ancient world but are also present on numerous occasions in the Hebrew Scriptures. Thus, so we find the special actions of God leading to human birth from the beginning with the very first humans, Adam and Eve, born of Divine action in a miraculous manner (Genesis 1: 26-27, 2: 21-23). Even Eve in turn on bearing Cain through entirely natural biological means proclaims, 'I have produced a man with the help of the Lord' (Genesis 4:1). The twins Esau and Jacob were born of the supposed barren Rebekah following the prayer of Isaac and subsequent divine intervention, while in the prediction that one will rule over the other there is a parallel with the pagan story where of the twins Romulus and Remus it is charged that the former will rule. Moses' birth as we have already seen, has a miracle attached to it in his being secreted in the bulrushes while Pharaoh sought to kill all the Hebrew children. A strong parallel with the birth of Jesus is found in the birth of Samson where, in like manner to the birth of Jesus, an angelic appearance to Manoah and his un-named wife leads to the birth of a child understood as a hero (Judges 13:2-24).

There are further instances of the divine understood to be participating in the birth of a man of God within the Hebrew Scriptures. In probably the best-known Isaac was miraculously born of Abraham and Sarah when the latter was very much post-menopausal (Genesis 18:10-14), while the birth of Samuel occurs when his mother Hannah apparently was barren (1 Samuel 1:4-20). Both acts, seen as results of God's miraculous intervention, result in children born destined for greatness and through whom the salvific action of God would be carried forward. Isaac was to be the one through whom the Jews would become the children of Abraham, while Samuel would act to anoint Israel's greatest

4: Virgin Mother!

king, David. Samuel's mother on learning of her upcoming miraculous birth bursts into an exclamatory song (1 Samuel 2:1-10) upon which that exclamatory song, the Magnificat, uttered by Mary, upon learning of her upcoming miraculous birth, is based (Luke 1:46-55).

Even in the Christian Scriptures the miraculous birth of Jesus is not the only or indeed the first miraculous birth with that honour falling to John the Baptist with his wondrous birth from the post-menopausal womb of Elizabeth (Luke 1:5-25). That birth parallels, as have just seen, those post-menopausal births of Isaac and Samuel. It also stands in Luke's gospel as a precursor with that which soon follows, the birth of Jesus. Of these post-menopausal births, it was believed by the biblical writers that sterility was caused by God closing the womb of a woman and being able to close it was equally able to reopen it at any time. This had been the case with Sarah (mother of Isaac), Hannah (mother of Samuel) and now, Elizabeth (mother of John the Baptist).

All these above births were miraculous and those born of such all had then a special role to play in the Divine plan. The birth of Jesus is however even more miraculous for nowhere else in the Jewish Scriptural tradition, contrary to the pagan traditions, do we find a miraculous birth coming without both parents being involved. Outside the Scriptures however, but still within the Jewish tradition, Philo speaks of the pregnancies of Sarah, Rebekah and Zipporah being due to an encounter with God (Cherubim 45:47) while Simon the Magician, who makes an appearance in the Christian Scriptures (Acts 8: 9-13), is another who was held in some quarters to be born of a virgin.

Luke as already stated gives far less weight to the virgin birth than does Matthew, only explicitly referring to it in two verses. According to Luke the actual event leading to the virgin birth saw Mary being overshadowed by the Holy Spirit (Luke 1:35) that linking, as I have said, to the divine presence known as the shekinah in the Jewish tradition. [4] Of course, this imagery of the Spirit hovering over or overshadowing has a parallel with the beginning of creation itself where the Spirit is described as 'brooding over the primal waters' (Genesis 1:2). We are being told here again of the absolute profundity of the birth of Jesus, understood here as nothing less than a new creation, a renewal of all things!

Further from within the Hebrew Scriptures there was another 'overshadowing' when the Spirit was said to have overshadowed the tabernacle (Exodus 40:35). The tabernacle offerings secured the relationship of those making offering to God so Luke is perhaps informing us that that relationship with God will now be established another way, through the child Mary will bear.

The other verse in which Luke alludes to the virgin birth is at the commencement of his genealogy where he states, 'Jesus when he began his ministry, was about 30 years of age, being the son (as was supposed) of Joseph' (Luke 3:23). The brackets may of course indicate a latter interpolation though there is no textual evidence for such.

In summary then, Luke in his account of the virgin birth quickly passes over it merely hinting at it. What he does say about it however informs us that this one as 'Son of God' is the inaugurator of a new creation. This may however simply represent Luke's theological line in general without a need to link it to a virgin birth which, given the evidence, could be a belief which Luke may not have really held. That would leave evidence for the virgin birth almost entirely with Matthew is something bound to shock many!

Ironically in subsequent theological use the virgin birth became used contrary to its original intent. Initially part of its intent had been to counter the arguments of the Docetists who insisted that God in Jesus had not taken human form but rather had only appeared to do so. The Docetists were part of a wider Gnostic movement, which following Platonic understanding judged material things, shown by their corruptibility, as being of essence evil, with only the non-material things, not subject to corruptibility, being good. The divine in Jesus, they asserted, could not therefore have taken corruptible human form but only appeared to do so. The main defence used by the early church against this was the argument that God had fully taken human form in Jesus. Initially this entailed Jesus as being assumed to have a natural birth like any other but over time as the status of Jesus rose, and in face of Jewish polemic as to his questionable birth, this entirely natural birth

4: Virgin Mother!

was not sufficient. The virgin birth narrative however still intended to affirm the fullness of divinity in human form. Unfortunately, it later came to become part of the Christian anti-flesh polemic.

When we remember that before this layer of the developing Christian tradition Jesus was only understood as being divine at his resurrection (Paul) or baptism (Mark) the virgin birth tradition served to push that divine presence more fully onto the human form right up to the point of that form's greatest vulnerability; infancy. It was in a sense an appreciation of the divine being present in enfleshed form, not in the full strength of adulthood, but rather at its weakest place. It stands then in this sense as being strongly affirmative of the flesh. As such the virgin birth was used by the early church father Ignatius of Antioch who in his disputation with the Docetists used it thus arguing Jesus, being born of a woman however miraculously, was one having full humanity.

Theologically I would argue however that the central Christian doctrinal need to have Jesus as one taking the fullness of human form to redeem humanity would logically preclude a half-way house stand whereby Jesus would have a birth qualitatively different from others, such as would be the case with a birth from a virgin. Born qualitatively different from all others, as he is in the Christian tradition, how in reality is he as one of us? The central Christian affirmation of Jesus' total identification with humanity as a human himself precludes him being ontologically (ontos = being) different, for if he is of a different order how is the crucial identity made that like us he is fully human and therefore able to redeem the human condition? In passing as well as voiding the virgin birth tradition on purely logical terms this would also likewise negate the Johannine solution of Jesus being the physical manifestation of the eternal 'logos' or Word for again having such pre-existence he would be ontologically of a different order from us. Indeed, such need of shared ontological status makes all statements as to the two natures of divinity and humanity being fully present in Jesus highly problematical if not nonsensical. How can one be fully human like any of us when so clearly different? Essentially what I am charging here is that no 'solution' can make sense of the central Christian affirmation that God is fully present in Jesus, be it the virgin birth tradition, the

Johannine logos tradition or the creedal dual nature of Christ claim if Jesus is held to be one in very essence with us as human beings. These all represent failures as attempts to logically explain a deep experienced belief that in Jesus one is met who is profoundly experienced as fully human but also divine. The Greek philosophical tradition however understood these categories, human and divine, as opposites and with an excluded middle, the two natures had to be held separate yet placed into one person. Far better would be to see humanity and divinity on one continuum rather than as opposed opposites. As such, a person in becoming more profoundly human would be understood as becoming more divine. Ultimately however such statements of faith as to the dual nature of Christ are best left intellectually as unsolvable conundrums and affirmed as experienced faith.

As already seen, contrary to how it had been used originally, in time the virgin birth became to be used in a manner highly depreciative of the flesh. Irenaeus (2nd century, there being much conjecture to the dates of both his birth and death) used it in developing his theory of recapitulation by which he saw the last Adam, Jesus, as truly human, winning back that paradisiacal state lost by the first Adam when in the flesh he sinned. The virgin birth he understood as being important in differentiating that latter Adam from the former for it removed him from being 'in the flesh.' This use of the virgin birth as a means of depreciating the flesh further developed in the 4th and 5th centuries with Ambrose (c. 340-397 CE) and then Augustine (354-430 CE) using it in their argument that human beings are born into 'original sin' with that sin having been passed on from the first sin of the couple in the Garden of Eden. The method of that sin being forwarded was through the carnal desire involved in that sexual intercourse necessary for all procreation, thereby meaning that the procreative act itself was the means of passing on that sin. Using modern parlance, it is as though the sin of the original couple is passed on as a genetic trait through the very act, sexual intercourse, necessary for procreation. The only way not to be caught up in this original sin would be to have a birth not involving sexual intercourse. This of course is, as seen, what is at the heart of

4: Virgin Mother!

the idea of the Immaculate Conception, the 19th century proclamation which finds its roots in Ambrose and Augustine.

With the Roman Empire Christianised in the early 4th century one result was the end of what was considered as being a higher path of faith; martyrdom. That led to a growing movement toward a living martyrdom in the denial of the natural human drives and needs. This ascetic ideal, usually centring on sexual denial, led to some retiring to the deserts and undertaking harsh ascetic practices while many women chose to live as virgins. Chastity became greatly prized and widely expected in the Christian community. Among the Nag Hammadi texts we find written, 'Woe to you who loved intimacy with womankind and polluted intercourse with it' (Thomas the Contender: 144). Probably composed in the early 3rd century this book exemplifies much of the writing of the time regarding sex. During the period from the 2nd to the 4th centuries a whole class of people even lived in marriage as brother and sister never consummating their marriage. This was particularly the case in the Syrian church where a whole group of men (benai qeiama) and women (benat qeiama), lived as chaste sons and daughters of the covenant. Often children were dedicated to God and left in monasteries to be educated and raised for this chaste life. Again, among the Syrians existed a group known as the Encratites who viewed virginity and chastity as being synonymous with the preaching of the gospel, with some teaching that Christ was bridegroom only to virgins and that baptism necessarily meant also embracing virginity and rejecting marriage. That through the virgin birth Christ was conceived without need for sexual intercourse meant that the virgin birth doctrine increasingly fuelled the gathering Christian aversion to such sex and anti-flesh polemic.

Of course, the growing belief and later subsequent doctrine of the virgin birth places women in an impossible bind in that they, unlike Mary, can never be 'ideal' for they are never able to fulfill the requisite role of being both mother and virgin! In the West, this has had a dramatic effect on female sexuality but also on how men view women.

The virgin birth represented that first step by which sexuality became progressively more and more understood as something at odds with the

Christian faith until the point where a type of what can only be called in the light of modern psychology, neuroticism, developed concerning sex, not only with the sexual act but all of those other things associated with it including gender preference and even the living in one's own enfleshed bodily form, becoming something despised to be finally cast off at death following which true disembodied life began. Sex became something dark and hidden and Christian history has shown the dangerous nature of this from castration in the early church through to violence against those who were seen to cause men to sin; women, homophobia, and the current plague of paedophilia in the Church.

Endnotes

1 B. Witherington III, article Birth of Jesus, Dictionary of Jesus and the Gospels, Joel B. Green, Scot Mc Knight, I. Howard Marshall (eds), Inter Varsity Press, Downers Grove, 1992: 64

2 Geza Vermes; The Changing Face of Jesus, Penguin, London, 2000:214

3 Judges 19: 16-30 This is a terrible story, one which is categorised by John Shelby Spong as being one of those stories he calls, 'the sins of Scripture.' In this story, a Levite is hosting a wayfarer and his concubine. The wayfarer is so handsome that a lust filled crowd is attracted outside his place. To assuage their lust and to protect his guest from homosexual rape he offers to send his virgin daughter and the wayfarer's concubine to them who are of course as we would put it in modern crude parlance, to be 'gang banged.' Rejecting the daughter due to some ethical scruples they take the concubine and clearly spend the night assuaging their lust. By morning she is unconscious or dead, the response then of the wayfarer being to put her on his ass, return home with her and then cut her in twelve pieces those pieces being sent all over Israel. The story ends with the only redeeming thing that, 'such a thing has never happened or been seen from the day that the people of Israel came up out of the land of Egypt until this day.' This passage is often used among others, to argue that the Bible views homosexuality negatively. Of course, in that cause it is only partially quoted with the grim recourse used to avoid homosexual rape omitted.

4 The presence of the Holy Spirit is a constant theme in Luke. In the Lukan infancy narrative John is full of the Holy Spirit while Jesus is conceived by the Holy Spirit. The Spirit is mentioned five times in Matthew, four times in Mark, four times in John and 12 times in Luke and 41 times in Luke's second volume, Acts.

5: MEET THE FAMILY

We have become so familiar with the Christmas stories that the figures begin to take a reality as though we know them as old personal friends who make an annual appearance. From Christmas cards and stained-glass windows, we are sure we cannot fail to recognise them; the shepherds, the wise men, the angels on high and of course Jesus' parents, Mary and Joseph. Of those parents, a familiar image is probably etched on our mind, the heavily pregnant Mary side-saddle on a camel or donkey with Joseph her husband walking beside her as they journey from Nazareth to Bethlehem to take part in Caesar's census.

It will surprise, if not shock most of us to know then that these so 'well-known' parents of Jesus don't enter the story until the eighth decade of the first century some 70 years after the events described in which they play their largest role. That not so grand entry to the story is made in Mark's gospel and then only one of the actors, Mary, is introduced with Joseph having to wait until further time passes.

We first meet Mary in Mark, along with the rest of her children, Jesus' siblings, not however in a favourable light with the references in that gospel regards Mary and the family all being pejorative. In their initial appearance Mary and the siblings are shown wishing to grab their son and brother, the busy itinerant preacher, and take him home for they have received reports that, 'he is beside himself' (Mark 3: 21). When the rest of that episode was picked up in the later synoptics, this deeply pejorative view of his family was expunged. That is understandable because by the time of the writings of Matthew and Luke they, as the holy family, have arrived at a status too high for them to be so strongly denigrated, though as we shall see some of the rejection by the Markan Jesus of his family will continue into Matthew's gospel. To return to Mark's account, for their concern regarding Jesus' psychological state the family are given short shrift by Jesus. When some of the crowd mention that his worried family is waiting for him outside Jesus' retort is, '"Who are my mother and my brothers?" And on looking around on those who sat about him (i.e. the crowd listening to his preaching), he said, 'here are my mother and my brothers! Whoever does the will of God is my brother, and sister, and mother'" (Mark 3:31-35). Strangers who do the will of God are seemingly closer to Jesus than his own kith and kin. On another occasion after opponents of Jesus have raised his familial links the low esteem in which Jesus holds his family is again clearly evidenced when of them he says, 'a prophet is not without honour, except in his own country and among his own kin, and in his own house' (Mark 6:3-6). Of course, this is in response to the questioning of Jesus' legitimacy by his opponents following their announcement of him as, 'the carpenter, son of Mary.' This identification was highly unusual for it was always the patrilineal line rather than the matrilineal line which was mentioned in these cases. What was been clearly and crudely said is, 'we don't know who the father is of this child whom we therefore consider to be illegitimate; a bastard' that last word catching the crudity of their charge. Such brazen questioning of Jesus' legitimacy is too much for Matthew so when he comes to lift this verse from Mark in his account he changes the wording of the charge from the crowd to, 'is not this the carpenter's son? Is not his mother Mary?' (Matthew 13:55) thereby providing paternity for Jesus by changing the reference of carpenter from one being directed toward Jesus to instead now being one directed at Joseph. By so doing he takes the sting out of the crowd's charge. Joseph, we shall find is introduced by Matthew into the story as a defence against this sort of charges to do with Jesus' paternity and therefore legitimacy. Mark however knows of no Joseph.

Again, elsewhere in Mark's gospel the concept of family loyalty takes a beating when Jesus speaking to his disciples says, 'Truly I say to you, there is no one who has left house or brothers or sisters, or mother or father or children or lands for my sake and for the gospel, who will not receive a hundred-fold now in this time, houses and brothers and sisters and mothers and children and lands' (Mark 10: 29-31). This statement however sounds more like second-hand commentary from a church experiencing persecution for their following of Jesus, than the actual words of Jesus. If it were Jesus' actual own statement, then it sounds unattractively egotistical.

5: Meet the family

In passing it seems ironically strange that Jesus has become someone who in the eyes of many is the defender of the nuclear family! The Christian Right have developed a whole political agenda around rejecting any practice of human sexuality which represents an alternative to that style of family by predicating Jesus as one who stands for 'Christian family values' as though the categories 'Christian' and 'family' essentially belong together. The Jesus of the gospels however is certainly not the archetypal 'good Jewish boy' instead having little time for his family and 'family values.' Great religious leaders are imaged like that as concerns their family with the Buddha leaving his sleeping wife and infant child, sneaking out in the dead of night, to go off to seek enlightenment. The mundanity of family and familial responsibility is left behind by such figures.

Though as I have indicated he moderates it, echoes of Jesus' estrangement from his family and their lack of understanding concerning him continue in Matthew's gospel. Thus, Matthew has Jesus announce how he will set, 'a man against his father and a daughter against her mother, a daughter-in-law against her mother-in-law and one's foes will be members of one's own household. Whoever loves father or mother more than me is not worthy of me; and whoever loves son or daughter more than me is not worthy of me' (Matthew 10:34-37). I take the first part of this statement as something probably going back to Jesus, though more so to do with the message he preaches rather than of he himself, while the second part, which again I understand as unattractive coming from his lips, I see as commentary of the church in their lived experience in times of persecution. In such a context where the choice may be between loyalty to family and loyalty to Jesus Matthew is telling us where true allegiance and love should lie. Matthew also picks up Mark's account almost word for word, excluding only the slur to do with his birth, on that occasion we looked at previously when Jesus preaching is told that his family are waiting outside (Matthew 12:46-50). As in Mark's gospel in Matthew's gospel Jesus is hardly presented as a good family man.

What may particularly surprise us in reading Matthew's Christmas story is the place of Mary in it. She takes no active part, never being present as the subject but merely as one spoken about. She is given no personality or real presence and makes no decisions while also, contrary to Luke's gospel, she receives not a word of revelation. Essentially, she is a 'cardboard' figure. Once again, we don't perceive this as our minds have been too filled with a Mary drawn from Luke's gospel. Again, we find those blinkers are called for! In Matthew's nativity story, it is Joseph who is the subject, the active player and decision maker and the one who receives divine revelation. It is time to meet him.

When we meet Joseph in this gospel we are meeting him some 85 years after the events to which he is supposedly involved! Even then he makes a first act appearance only, appearing first in the Matthean and then later in the Lukan nativity stories before then vanishing from the rest of those gospels.

I believe that not only does our traditional image of Joseph need be called into question, but even his actual reality itself, for Joseph I contend, is entirely a creation of midrash. Let us turn now to look at him.

Most people will know of the often-dreaming Joseph of the Hebrew Scriptures, the one whose eleven jealous brothers sell off to a passing Egyptian trader. He dreams even more prolifically than the Joseph of the nativity story while also having the ability to interpret the dreams of others (Genesis 37:5, 9, 19, 40: 9-19, 41:1-36). That Joseph of old like that Joseph here also has a father called Jacob (Genesis 35:24 c.f. Matthew 1:16) while also the Joseph of old like Jesus' father saves the family by making a journey into Egypt, where of course he rises to power because of his ability to dream (Genesis 41:38). Here in our nativity gospel stories there is an obvious paralleling with the Joseph of the Hebrew Scriptures. Both are great dreamers, a means by which they receive divine revelation, both have fathers bearing the same name and both are forced to journey into Egypt so to save their family. There may be another connection in that the Joseph of old was one of the twelve brothers through whom was represented the 12 tribes of Israel while the Joseph of the infancy narrative is the one who, as 'father' in Matthew's theological schema, gives birth to a 'new Israel.'

As a creation of midrash from the Joseph of old this newer Joseph of the gospel narratives has not, I contend, the least jot of historical

5: Meet the family

existence. The only thing this newer Joseph, as distinct from the original Joseph, seemingly lacks is a coat of many colours!

Having seen the parallels and their role in the creation of Joseph let us more closely examine the role this 'figure' plays in Matthew's infancy narrative. In Joseph's first dream he is told that it is by the Holy Spirit that his betrothed Mary has been impregnated and that the name of the child to be born is to be Jesus. In the Ancient Near East, as in many ancient cultures names were crucially important. They defined the person so named and expressed the hope placed in them, meaning that in a sense one was defined by their name. The importance in the naming of a child is seen in Luke's gospel with the events, which we will later examine, concerning the naming of John the Baptist (Luke 1:57-66). The name Jesus, in Hebrew Yeshu or Yeshua, is a form of the name famous in the Hebrew Scripture, Joshua, the great hero who, after the death of Moses, had led the Hebrews into the Promised Land. It means 'God saves' and so Matthew adds, just in case you don't get it, in his commentary on this quotation, 'because he will save people from their sins' (Matthew 1:21). We may note in passing that nowhere in Jewish thought is there the idea that the Messiah will save people from sin. The salvation wrought by Joshua of course was far earthier than that, being a bloody military conquest of an already inhabited land largely carried out by butchering its inhabitants. Such a militarist power understanding of the messianic role as one bringing retributive justice, rather than anything to do with the Messiah forgiving sins primarily shaped the Jewish understanding of the messianic role.

Why does Joseph need to be created? The need is clear, for as we have seen there was a great scandal and charge first by the opponents of Jesus, and then later by the opponents of the early church concerning the legitimacy of Jesus' birth and as we have already seen scandal around one's birth up until very recent times has counted for much. It most certainly would disqualify one from being the Messiah. It is possible even to see in Mary's calling of herself in the Magnificat as being of 'lowly estate' a reference to the illegitimate nature of the child she is carrying for in a traditional society there was no lower estate than to be with child outside wedlock. It seems that in defending Jesus' paternity there are two responses by his followers, one being to construct Joseph as being the putative father, the second being the development of the virgin birth tradition. In any case a combination of the virgin birth and the creation of Joseph as 'father' seemingly deflected the awkward questions and allowed the question of Jesus' paternity to be 'solved.'

There is possibly another reason for the creation of Joseph. After the death of King Solomon some 900 years before, the 12 tribes of the Kingdom of Israel had divided into two. In the south was Judah dominated by the tribe of that name, while in the north were the ten tribes, properly called Israel, dominated by the tribes of Ephraim and Manasseh. It was held that Jacob, father of the original Joseph had two principal wives, Leah the mother of Judah associated with the tribe of that name, and Rachel, the mother of Joseph, associated with the tribes of Ephraim and Manasseh. Matthew's genealogy as we have seen centres on David strongly associated with Judah in which he was believed to have constructed his capital, Jerusalem. By bringing a Joseph, associated with the northern tribes into the picture Matthew can thus present Jesus as one who, like David, central in Matthew's understanding, brings the two parts, Israel and Judah together. As such he is the founder of a new Israel. It is only right of course then for Jesus to be born out of Joseph's line, Joseph being associated with the north, for it is from out of Galilee that Jesus comes and as we shall see was almost certainly born.

Further the creation of Joseph called by Matthew 'the son of David' (Matthew 1:20) serves again to firmly place Jesus in the line of David. This is crucially important as it was universally expected that the Messiah would come out of David's line.

This created Joseph takes off so that John in his gospel, never mentioning the virgin birth, simply speaks of Joseph as the natural father of Jesus (John 1:45, 6:42). There he is called a 'teknon' which in Greek probably means 'craftsman' though there are possible links through the supposed Aramaic lying behind the Greek to his being a scholar. The vast weight of evidence falls however on the former. This is something far different from the classic picture of Joseph being like some type of modern day tradesman carpenter. The carpentry trade today is a skilled trade and is amply rewarded. Joseph however as a 'teknon' lay near the bottom of the socio-economic pile. The economy of Jesus' epoch was one almost totally agrarian and as such prosperity lay in the land. We know that increasingly in the time of Jesus more and more people were falling into debt and were therefore being driven off the land, which was becoming more and more concentrated into fewer and fewer hands. The Torah had been written of course to preclude this happening for within it there were all sorts of strictures on use of the land and the enslavement of those in debt, slavery after-all being highly repugnant to those whose identity was so linked to their being freed from slavery in Egypt. The Torah however was being increasingly disregarded, while of course the Roman overlords paid it little heed. Those whose debts were insurmountable had as a first resort the recourse of selling their land and if the new owner was agreeable becoming share-croppers or serfs on that land they once owned. Of course, often that was only a temporary resort for, as with current day sharecroppers, they had to give a large percentage of their crop to the owner of the land as rent meaning debts would pile up even faster. Finally, as a last resort they may have to sell even their family and themselves into slavery. If you think of the stories Jesus tells you will find plenty of allusions to this economic reality (Matthew 18:23-35, 19:16-23, 20:1-16, 21:33-41, Luke 7:41-43, 12:13-21, 16:19-31). Probably the best-known example is the story Jesus tells of the prodigal son, where even a son decides to sell himself to his father because of debt owed to him (Luke 15: 11-32). If a son considers selling himself to his father, we can surmise how common was this selling oneself into slavery. Jesus' family, being of the landless class, could represent those who had been driven off their land as source of wealth either as owners or tenants, and given such it is highly likely they lay very near the bottom of the economic pile. Little wonder Jesus tells stories from the underside and prays a prayer asking only for 'daily bread' for thinking about bread for tomorrow was a step too far for those caught in such grinding poverty.

    In Matthew we clearly find Joseph as the central protagonist in the infancy story in contrast to Luke's gospel where that role clearly falls to Mary. Thus, in Matthew's gospel it is Joseph who names the child, while as we shall see in Luke's gospel Mary does, while the revelation of the birth and its significance in this gospel falls to Joseph, whereas in Luke's gospel that will fall to Mary. Whatever his presumed role in Jesus' actual biological birth, Joseph, in Matthew's gospel plays the role of the traditional Jewish family patriarch very much but having played his role he then disappears from the story.

In passing Joseph could still be of use some two millennia later when the Roman Catholic Church found his working roots to be of use in instituting St Joseph the Worker Day on May 1, an attempt to steal a march on the Communists in co-opting May Day.

If it is Matthew in his nativity account who creates for us a Joseph with whom we have become familiar, it is Luke who creates for us the Mary we so know. We need to remember however that by the time of Luke's writing we are even further temporally removed again, perhaps a century or more, from the actual events being described. The historicity of his account must then be even more questionable. However, having said that let us now turn to examine Luke's account.

Mary in Luke's gospel is encountered as one overcome with fear when the annunciation of the angel is given to her (Luke 1:29), is related to Elizabeth mother of John the Baptist, with whom she will have her miraculous birth story compared, presented as the singer of the Magnificat (Luke 1:46-55), as one pondering these various miraculous events in her heart (Luke 2:19) and finally as one travelling with Joseph and the family for Passover when Jesus was 12 years old, having need to rebuke her young son for remaining there after the family had left for home (Luke 2:41-48). She then disappears from the Luke's writings until she reappears in a brief note in passing at the very conclusion of the gospel where the resurrection of her son is announced to her among others (Luke 24:10) after which we learn in Luke's second volume Acts, that she has become a believer, along with the siblings of Jesus, as part of the infant church (Acts 1:14). One of those siblings, James, we are told, has become the leader of the Jerusalem church (Acts 15:13-21), a church in which we find elsewhere others of Jesus' brothers holding significant places (I Corinthians 9:5). From Paul, we find the leadership role of

James confirmed though clearly James and Paul are trenchant opponents in a deep conflict as to the meaning of the faith (Galatians 2:1-10).

Mary is best known for her joyous ecstatic poetical exclamation in the Magnificat (Luke 1: 46-55) so called because Jerome's translated Latin text begins 'Magnificat anima mea Dominum' (My soul magnifies the Lord). Of course, the original words are poetic in form in the Greek of the Christian Scriptures rather than in the spoken Aramaic in which Mary would have of course uttered any such words. These words are clearly a creation of Luke in Greek rather than those spoken in Aramaic by Mary with the sentiments contained therein reflective of Luke's theology rather than being any actual utterance of Mary. Further, who would have known or remembered any words spoken so long before by one of such 'low estate?'

In the Hebrew Scriptures both men and women often sang hymns of praise in response either to God's generosity or display of greatness to them. We hear such hymnic praise from Moses (Exodus 15: 1-8), Miriam (Exodus 15: 19-21), Deborah (Judges 5:1-31), Asaph (I Chronicles 16:7-36), Hannah (I Samuel 2: 1-10), and from the Psalms (particularly Psalms 33, 47, and 136). The Magnificat strongly draws as we have already seen, on one of these, the Song of Hannah. In that song and in the Magnificat both women, Hannah and Mary, after giving birth to children destined for greatness, extol God's greatness, are called God's 'handmaiden' or 'maidservant' (I Samuel 1:11, Luke 1:48) while each acknowledge that God's purposes will be accomplished through the births of their respective children (I Samuel 1:11, 21, 28, Luke 1:32-35). As Samuel, born of Hannah was consecrated to the Lord as a priest likewise is Jesus so consecrated. The role of a priest was to offer sacrifice to God to bring about God's continued blessing and in a radically different manner Jesus acting as 'priest' will make sacrifice, namely himself, to secure God's blessing.

That blessing by God as given in Mary's song clearly has social ramifications in its bringing of a new age of justice and equity. Much of the poem is written in a chiasmic style, a style where an attribute is paired with its opposite e.g. mighty/humble, rich/hungry. Such reversal motifs are seen often in the Hebrew Scriptures (I Samuel 2: 7-8, Job

5:8-11 Isaiah 2:11, 5:15-16, Ezekiel 17:24, 21:25-26) with Jesus himself several times uttering one which has become almost synonymous with him in many people's minds, 'the first shall be last and the last shall be first.' This chiasmic style is used here to indicate the advent of this new messianic age, 'He has scattered the proud in the imagination of their hearts, has put down the mighty from their thrones, and exalted those of low degree; has filled the hungry with good things and the rich he has sent empty away' (Luke 1:51-53). In this section the past tense is used by the evangelist in the belief that even in the annunciation these things are already coming to pass.

In picking up this theme the Magnificat draws on that concern for the poor, understood by the Hebrew word 'anawin,' as the totally destitute, something well attested in the Hebrew Scriptures where the Divine concern for the poor, orphan, lowly and hungry is often seen (Deuteronomy 15:7-11 Leviticus 19:9-18, Isaiah 1:12-17, Amos 2:6-7 et. al). In Luke's gospel, this theme continues in the programmatic statement Jesus makes for himself in the synagogue at the commencement of his ministry (Luke 4:18-19) and in Luke's beatitudes, much less known than those found in Matthew, chiasmic in style where each beatitude offered to the lowly is contrasted with a woe directed at the powerful (Luke 6:20-26).

In looking at Luke's infancy story you may note I have not at all mentioned Joseph. That is simply because if Mary had no real presence in Matthew's account, Joseph in this gospel is even more of a 'bit-player.' He had one of those roles you hated receiving, while others were the stars, in the school play.

We find then those so familiar well-known parents of Jesus are not quite as we believe them to be. Mary doesn't appear anywhere in the early Christian tradition until the time of the writing of Mark's gospel some 70 years after the time in which she supposedly played such a central role. Of course, in Mark's gospel, without any nativity story, we find nothing of what was to become that central role, the birthing of Jesus. Instead she and the family are mentioned only in passing and the appearance they make at that time, hardly flattering, is one which places them squarely in the camp of those who just 'don't get' Jesus. Mary is still but a 'cardboard' figure in her central casting role, the birthing of Jesus in Matthew's gospel some 15 years later. Despite her mere bystander role in the Matthean infancy narrative she still would have witnessed all the incredible things allegedly to do with the birth of Jesus, but her knowing supposedly such of her son is at total odds wither being the uncomprehending one presented in the rest of Matthew's gospel! Even as late as the time of the writing of Luke Mary and her family outside of the nativity stories continue to be those who fall into the non-believing camp when it comes to Jesus, this despite how she is presented in the Lukan nativity account as the recipient of incredible revelation. In conclusion, we ought to note that in John's independent gospel tradition Mary and the family are presented likewise negatively, though only in passing, as non-believers for we are told, 'not even his brothers had faith in him' (John 7:5). As we have seen only later, after the time of Jesus, do Mary and the family come to believe and become prominent within the infant church. Given this prominence, using the criteria of embarrassment, we can confidently say that during the time of Jesus' ministry his family's actual role was that of being uncomprehending or even oppositional for otherwise this embarrassment would have been covered up, but seemingly so well-known was the family attitude during the time of Jesus' ministry that was not possible.

The uncomprehending or even oppositional nature of Mary and the siblings of Jesus along with his wider kith and kin in the Scriptures outside of the nativity narratives clearly shows that these stories have no credible historical basis. After all, how strange it is, if we are to believe the nativity accounts in Matthew's gospel where even wise men from the East having followed a miraculous celestial sign come to worship Jesus, that Mary and her family later during the time of his ministry seemingly have no understanding of him and his special role, a role which had also been made so clear by no less than an angel appearing thrice in Joseph's dreams! Turning to the Lukan nativity narrative, could not Mary remember the angel's annunciation and her poetic exclamatory response? What of Elizabeth's unborn infant jumping in the womb as a sign of the likewise unborn one greater than him? If all those things in the Matthean and Lukan nativity accounts had really happened it is hardly likely that Jesus' parents would not have suspected that there was something special about their child, that they had one special kid! In reality however, none of those incredible events ever happened.

Mary was no doubt a mother probably mystified and afraid of the actions of her somewhat strange 'God intoxicated' son Jesus, for she, no doubt knowing the harsh nature of Roman rule, whether directly or through Herodian proxies, must have feared as to where her son's actions would bring him. It is likely she would have been familiar with the fate of other rabble rousing prophetic figures challenging the establishment and would have had no desire for that same end for her son. Like the mother of Brian in Monty Python's 'The Life of Brian', a comical parody of the Christ story, she must have wished the crowds would all just go away, and that Jesus would come to his senses, come home and be like others. As for the father, 'Joseph' lacking actual flesh is entirely a literary creation drawn by midrash from that fellow dreaming Joseph of long ago. His creation, along with the virgin birth, is a means by which the early followers of Jesus respond to the slander regarding the paternity of the one they follow. As such another part of our well-loved Christmas story falls away.

6: O LITTLE TOWN OF NAZARETH

One of those things we feel most certain about is that Jesus was born in the town of Bethlehem just a few kilometres from Jerusalem itself. Bethlehem of course would make a most auspicious birthplace for Jesus in that it was universally believed that the longed-for Messiah would come from that place. Again, we feel we 'know' the story, the holy family making a long journey, so to fulfil the demands of the Roman census, from Nazareth to that town of Bethlehem where upon arriving they could find no room in which to give birth to the infant Mary was carrying, instead having to make do with a stable with the animals surrounding. Of course, we have already found that such assumed 'knowledge' in the Christmas narratives is for the most part lacking factually.

Turning now to the place and manner of Jesus' birth we find yet again that we are dealing with pious fiction rather than fact. So well do we 'know' this story of Mary and Joseph needing to journey from their home-town Nazareth to a place in which they did not reside, Bethlehem, we fail to recognise that this is only one of the two traditions, that of Luke, while Matthew has Jesus' parents not as visitors to Bethlehem but rather as residents of that place!

Jesus was almost certainly not born in Bethlehem but rather to the north in Galilee in a town called Nazareth. Indeed, the idea that Jesus was born in Bethlehem doesn't enter the Christian tradition until 80-90 years after his birth, Matthew being the first to have him born in there. There is no Bethlehem tradition present in the earliest Christian writings of Paul or Mark, it just being simply assumed that Jesus was a Galilean. Both before and after the Bethlehem birth enters the tradition, Jesus is always associated with that place in which he was almost certainty born, being known as 'Jesus of Nazareth' or 'the Nazarene' (Mark 1:24, 6:1-6, 16:6, Matthew 21:11, 26:71, Luke 4:16, 18:37, 24:19, John 1:45, 18:5), while the earliest followers of Jesus were called Nazarenes (Acts 24:5).

The town of Nazareth in Galilee had no place in the holy tradition and was what we would call in Australia, 'beyond the black stump.' It was 'Nowheresville' or 'Hicksville' never mentioned in the Hebrew

Scriptures, and even after the birth of Jesus remains insignificant, not being mentioned by the contemporary Jewish historian Josephus, nor in the later Mishnah and Talmud. Given then that Nazareth was no place in which to have a Messiah born both Matthew and Luke conspire to have Jesus born in that far more auspicious location of Bethlehem though their means of getting him born there, as seen, are at total odds.

Bethlehem of course was auspicious for being King David's town and given that the anticipated Messiah was to be born of David's line it made sense then to have Jesus born in David's town. In this both gospel writers drew from the Hebrew Scriptures wherein it is stated 'David was the son of an Ephrathite in Judah named Jesse.' (1 Samuel 16:1, 17:12), an Ephrathite being an inhabitant of Bethlehem. Luke makes this Davidic connection explicit by having it stated in the angelic annunciation Jesus will inherit the throne of David (Luke 1:32). David's throne had been long empty since the 6th century BCE when the conquering Babylonians had killed all the heirs of King Zedekiah before plucking out his eyes and marching him into captivity (2 Kings 25:7). The Messiah it was widely expected would come as the truly anointed king reinstituting David's line and restoring Israel to greatness.

The terms Messiah and king are basically interchangeable, along with that of the 'anointed one.' Each king at coronation was anointed and of each it was hoped that they would be the Messiah, understood as the true successor of David. These coronation rites and the hopes contained within them can be seen in numerous Psalms, known as the royal Psalms (Psalm 2, 18, 20, 21, 45, 72, 101, 110, 132). That messianic hope and hunger grew following the Babylonian exile, with a series of weak kings, not out of David's line, sitting on the throne, and by the time of Jesus in an Israel under Roman yoke had in many quarters become white hot. Thus, roughly contemporary with Jesus there were numerous messianic figures, each with their followers believing the one they were following to be the one come to be the Messiah. Among them were Simon of Peraea, Judas (not Iscariot), Theudas, a figure called 'the Egyptian,' Athronges and John the Baptist while later came the rebel leader Simon bar Kockhba.

6: O little town of Nazareth

Let us now examine how the two evangelists, in their totally divergent ways, get the holy family to that requisite town. As said Matthew's lesser known schema will probably surprise us given that we have become so familiar with Luke's account of having the holy family journey to Jerusalem for a census. That story is so at the heart of our Christmas folk tradition that Matthew's account with Joseph and Mary being denizens of Bethlehem and having their child in their hometown is completely overlooked. Far from their toil of journeying being a thing preceding the birth as in Luke, with a long journey to Bethlehem, in this gospel Joseph and Mary's troubles begin following the birth where, because of Herod's evil scheming, the holy place becomes full of peril and they are forced to make the arduous journey fleeing as refugees out of Bethlehem to Egypt. That flight of course becomes part of the 'known' story meaning that the family are understood to have had two journeys, one to Bethlehem before the birth and another fleeing it following the birth. In the linking these two stories it is clear to see how seamlessly we move from one gospel to the other in constructing our accepted Christmas story. From Luke we have the journey and then move to Matthew to have Herod's pogrom and then the subsequent flight to Egypt!

Luke has the family correctly I believe (the last correct thing in this account however), living in Nazareth and so has the problem of finding a means of getting them to the holy town, the expected birthplace of the Messiah. He does so by a fantastic method, creating an empire-wide census for which elsewhere we have found no record. Having arrived in Bethlehem their troubles are over, and Luke has them remain there publicly going up to the Temple to carry out all the requisite rituals associated with the birth of a son. Unlike in Matthew's account there is no pogrom carried out by Herod causing the family to flee to Egypt but instead the they are able to securely remain in Bethlehem even travelling openly several times into Jerusalem.

Now of course both stories are equally quite incredible if we are to take them literally. Of Matthew's gospel are we to believe that Herod, who as we shall see, had managed to secure his position by skilfully playing off some of the most powerful men in Rome, now feared a peasant child (Matthew 2:3)? Herod would not have even known of the unrecorded birth of this peasant child much less feared him! Further even if he did have such fear this ruthless but skilful ruler would have found better methods with which to deal with this fear than an unnecessary brutal pogrom of male infants.

As for Luke's gospel likewise are we to understand that the holy family journey to Jerusalem for an otherwise unheard-of empire wide census? Supposedly they are called to go there because they are out of David's line. Given David lived some 1,000 years previously just about everyone would have had some Davidic lineage. Did they all travel to Bethlehem? No wonder there was 'no room in the inn.' Further are we to believe that the ruthlessly efficient Romans called a census in such an illogical manner creating social, political and economic chaos across their empire? Of course, this census is constructed by Luke out of that theological project he shared with Matthew, the need to have the Messiah born in the propitious town of Bethlehem with its long sacred tradition, and he will use any means to get his birth to be there, covering up the reality that Jesus' actual birth was in a place, Nazareth, without any sacred status. Luke's method is the census whereby the family journey temporarily to Bethlehem before returning home to Nazareth. Matthew's method is to have Jesus' family living in Bethlehem before having them move to Nazareth via a long detour to Egypt. Both enable Jesus to be born in the messianic town of King David while acknowledging as everyone knew, that Jesus was a Nazarene out of Galilee.

As we have repeatedly seen, our gospels, especially the infancy narratives, are less shaped by history than they are by the Hebrew Scriptures through the a-historical processes of midrash. It is again to those Scriptures that we must turn to find the roots for this need for the birth to take place in the royal town. The passage in Hebrew Scripture which most determines this birthplace is from Micah with Matthew even quoting it to seal his case for the birthplace. 'Bethlehem, Ephrathah, you are one of the smallest towns in Judah, but out of you I will bring a ruler for Israel, whose family line goes back to ancient days' (Micah 5:2 c.f. Matthew 2:6). Of course, for Micah writing in the eighth century BCE the prophecy had absolutely nothing to do with Jesus.

6: O little town of Nazareth

Rather it was meant as a word of comfort, promising that following the destruction of both the northern kingdom Israel, as well as much of the Judean south by the Assyrian invaders, a divine intervention would see the restoration of the nation with the temple rebuilt on Zion with a ruler Micah believed who would be born in Bethlehem conquering the Assyrians. Interestingly Matthew cuts the quotation short for the rest of it would well suit his cause for Micah goes on to speak of how this ruler will rule a people in exile, with strength, resulting in peoples from all over the earth acknowledging him. Israel at the time of Jesus' birth could be said to be 'living in exile' while it was subjugated under the Roman Empire, and Matthew clearly understands Jesus as being acknowledged from all over the earth as ruler, as indeed he was by his followers from all parts of the Empire by the time of Matthew's writing.

This understanding of the place of the Messiah's birth as something being prophesied in the Scriptures was not only confined to the early church, with others also appropriating such prophecy for their use. Ironically among those others supposedly was Herod who has his scribes search the Hebrew Scriptures finding of course the quotation from Micah for the birthplace of the Messiah so that he too 'could go and worship him' (Matthew 2:3-5). To Herod and his rule, we shall turn later.

As to the actual historical reality of the birthplace of Jesus, the writer of the fourth gospel, John, again lets the cat out of the bag. Knowing nothing of the late developing Bethlehem tradition associated with Jesus, in his gospel he has the crowds charge, 'The Messiah will not come from Galilee! The Scriptures says that the Messiah will be a descendant of King David and will be born in Bethlehem, the town where David lived' (John 7:41-42). There could hardly be stronger evidence, both to the intentional creation of the Bethlehem birth tradition but also to the reality of Jesus' birthplace being Nazareth. Everyone, we are told, knew that it was in Nazareth that Jesus was born and each knowing that knew that Jesus being born there rather than in Bethlehem could not the Messiah so long expected. The cry here was clearly meant to seal the case for Jesus' opponents that he, rather than being the Messiah was an imposter. It would seem precisely to counter such a critique of the crowds that the tradition had begun in Matthew and Luke to move the birth of the one claimed to be Messiah to the Davidic centre of Bethlehem, though John himself clearly never sees any need to do so.

Let us turn now to more closely examine the Matthean story. In this gospel, as we have found, Jesus is born in Bethlehem, the town we are told in which his parents reside. Around Jesus' birth however is a danger associated with King Herod, who upon learning of the birth from visiting wise men from the east who have followed a star, feels sufficiently threatened to seek to kill this one he judges to be a threat to his throne. Astrological phenomena, as we have seen, were often associated with the birth of royalty or great figures in the ancient world. His plans are thwarted by those dreams of Joseph of which we have spoken. Joseph having already in one dream being told the manner of Mary's pregnancy now finds his dreams come into play for a second time, this time giving warning of Herod's tyrannical plans. In those plans of Herod, we find yet another example of midrash, a link being made to the like birth of Moses amid the threatening atmosphere caused by Pharaoh's orders. Herod is thus presented as one like Pharaoh, endeavouring to put a stop to the divine story by the mass massacre of innocent male infants (Exodus 1:15-22, c.f. Matthew 2:16-18).

One of those marked for slaughter under Pharaoh's policy was Moses, who as we know miraculously escapes (Exodus 1:21-2:10). Now likewise Jesus miraculously escapes the consequences of such tyranny. These Moses parallels continue in Matthew's gospel, being particularly strong around the commencement of Jesus' ministry. Thus Matthew has Jesus open the Jordan, as did Moses the Red Sea, though in Jesus' case it is in the act of being baptised (Matthew 3: 13-17), spend 40 days in the desert in like manner to Moses' 40 years (Matthew 4:1-11), before giving a new law, in likewise location as Moses received the old law, on a mountain (Exodus 20:1-17, Deuteronomy 5:1-21, Matthew 5:1-48 c.f. Luke's plain, Jesus having come down from a mountain Luke 6: 12, 17-49). [1]

For Matthew, these parallels are drawn because he understands Jesus, like Moses, as being a great teacher and law giver with each opposed, even from their births, by the tyranny of those who rule them. To an old law judged oppressive they each give a new law, Moses the Torah so contrary to the Egyptian law, and Jesus, in Matthew's understanding a new law tightening the Torah. In the Hebrew Scriptures Egypt's Pharaoh is the evil figure, enforcing an oppressive law, which necessitates the exodus of Israel out of Egypt to the 'Promised Land,' where the children of Israel are to live under a new liberating law, the Torah, centred on justice. Now Jesus according to Matthew, like Moses, will lead a new exodus into a new and liberating law away from that which is judged to be oppressive associated with the Pharisees (Matthew 23:1-33).

We should note that, despite much Christian commentary viewing it as an oppressive instrument to be countered by Christian grace, the way Jews understand the Torah to this very day is that it is something viewed with great love, held to be a freeing liberating thing remembered and celebrated, especially each Shabbat (Sabbath). The common Christian understanding of the Torah, as something oppressive finds its roots in the writings of Paul who given his personal journey writes of it highly pejoratively. Contrary to Paul however, Matthew's gospel presents Jesus is one who tightens the strictures of the Law, of which not an iota will be done away with (Matthew 5:18). He does so in attempting to get at the real heart of the Law, which he clearly judges as something liberating. In this he is contrasted with the Pharisees who are presented as enforcing the Law in an oppressive manner, but of course, given Matthew's theological project, this is far more a caricature of the Pharisees than any actuality.

Matthew is suggesting here in his nativity story that the event which is taking place represents an entirely new exodus with Jesus being either a new Moses or perhaps one even representing Israel itself. With grim intended irony, here it is the evil actions, not of a foreign king which lead to an exodus to Israel but rather the evil actions of a Jewish king Herod, whose rule necessitate an exodus out of Israel to Egypt as a type of 'reverse exodus.' Thus, the sting in the tail that Matthew gives us is that Israel has become so corrupt that the exodus must be reversed, out of Israel now to find refuge in Egypt, that place which for the Jewish people was remembered as the place of bondage (Exodus 20:2). The place from which they escaped to freedom, now becomes the place of refuge. Pharaoh was understood as the archetypal tyrannical leader who had kept the Hebrews enslaved, but now it is Egypt which offers freedom while it falls to the Jewish king, Herod to be the one working evil.

Despite a reputation as a place of bondage Egypt was a traditional place of flight with Abraham (Genesis 12:10) and Jeremiah, whom Matthew quoting so clearly has in mind (Matthew 2:17-18), both finding safety there, while Jeroboam (1 Kings 11:40, 12:2) and Uriah (Jeremiah 26:21) are also forced to into exile to that land. Even Moses himself found refuge there (Exodus 4:19-20).

In the similar vein, again deliberately paradoxically, in Matthew's gospel we find that while the leadership of Israel, King Herod, stands opposed to the actions of God it is foreigners, represented by the wise men, astrologers, from the east, who are the ones who pay homage to this one of God. Thus the foreign wise men reading the stars accept Jesus, while Herod reading, or more so misreading for dark purposes, the Hebrew Scriptures, not only refuses to accept Jesus as Messiah but is prepared to carry out the most horrific act to do away with the one through whom God is acting. Again, Matthew reverses everything in his directed attack at the Jewish establishment.

Of course, one can't help but wonder why Herod didn't simply have some spies follow the wise men after they had left, to find the specific child, rather than relying on their promise to return. That simple action would have precluded the need to conduct a massacre and would surely have nabbed the pretender in a simple action.

Having been warned in a dream of Herod's plan to massacre all male infants under two, Joseph leads the family into refuge in Egypt in like manner as had the Joseph of old led to the people of Israel to spend time in that land. Given that Matthew understands Jesus as symbolic of a new Israel, Joseph here like that Joseph of old, is the means by which the founder of this new Israel finds refuge in Egypt.

Matthew then takes yet another opportunity to use the Hebrew Scriptures to draw yet another parallel, quoting Jeremiah 31:15 to tell us of the weeping of 'Rachel' following Herod's massacre. Rachel was viewed as the mother figure of Israel and here she is weeping for her children, who like Jesus, were killed or driven into exile, in this case to Babylon in the 6th century BCE with the reference to Ramah present because it was at that place the populace had been gathered in preparation for exile to their conqueror's homeland. It was there that Rachel had her grave from which it was believed 'she weeps to this day' according to this episode in Matthew's gospel. As the Israel of old was forced into exile so too is Jesus, in whom is founded a new Israel. The exile however this time as we have seen is not caused by a foreign empire but rather comes from the hand of the Jewish ruler, one prepared even to carry out a massacre to achieve his goal! With Israel fallen this low in Matthew's estimation little wonder he has Rachel still weeping.

In the final episode of Matthew's Christmas story, the holy family is able to return to Israel from Egypt, and once more we are told of how this is all in accord with Scripture. Thus, we read, 'I have called my Son out of Egypt' (Hosea 11:1 c.f. Matthew 2:15) and that now it is safe to return, 'for all those who were seeking your life are dead' (Exodus 4:19 c.f. Matthew 2:20). That they are to return to Israel is known again through one of Joseph's dreams, this being the third time that God has thus spoken to him. The wording of the angel to Joseph in his dream is the same here as it was in his original dream where he had been told to take the child and flee to Egypt. 'Rise, take the child and his mother' (Matthew 2:13 c.f. 2:20). This time however, he is to 'rise' and return to Israel.

On returning Matthew has them go to the place where he has Jesus born; Bethlehem. Seemingly however, the revelation in this dream was not fully communicated or received, because a supplementary dream is needed once the family return to Judea to get them away from what in Matthew's gospel is their hometown of Bethlehem and have them now move instead to Nazareth in Galilee (Matthew 2:19-23). Matthew gives his reasoning as to why Jesus' family must move to that final abode by telling us that Archelaus, the son of Herod, was reigning in Judea, conveniently overlooking the fact that another son of Herod, Herod Antipas, was on the throne in Galilee. One may wonder as to the logic given that Judea was not safe because a son of Herod ruled there as to how Galilee where another son ruled was safer. It need be remembered however that the rule of Archelaus was particularly tyrannical in nature to the extent that the Romans chose to remove him from the throne after some 10 years and impose direct rule through prefects and procurators, whereas his brother Antipas ruled for thrice that time. Herod Antipas however was no benevolent ruler and Matthew himself tells us that it was he who had the head of Jesus' close associate, John the Baptist on a plate (Matthew 14:1-12).

Nonetheless Matthew shows such confidence in his solution that he concludes, 'he shall be called a Nazarene.' Though Matthew claims prophetic background for this quote it nowhere features within the Hebrew Scriptures. This non-appearance is not unexpected for as we have seen Nazareth was totally outside the holy tradition and therefore unmentioned, so clearly Matthew is stretching reality by seeking a Scriptural basis for the Nazareth location. In doing this it is possible that Matthew is thinking of Isaiah 11 where there is spoken of one, seemingly a messianic figure who, 'shall not judge by what his eyes see or decide by what his ears hear, but with righteousness shall judge the poor and decide with equity for the poor of the earth.' He does so as a branch out of Jesse, the father of David (Isaiah 11:1). In Hebrew, the word for branch is 'nezar' which may have reminded Matthew of Nazareth. Remember, as we have seen, in written Hebrew the vowels are absent, so the two words look to be more similar than they would for us. In the choice of readings for the lectionary, or cycle of recited readings, the church understands this passage from Isaiah as pointing to the Nazarene by placing these readings together. Jesus is elsewhere understood as a branch out of Jesse's tree (Acts 13:22-23, Romans 15:12).

Thus, we arrive at the completion of Matthew's schema of having Jesus born in Bethlehem, the auspicious place, then of having him like Moses and indeed Israel of old, both to which he desires to have Jesus paralleled, make an exodus journey, before finally having him end up in the place, Nazareth, from which everyone knew he came.

Let us now turn to Luke's gospel. Luke has as we have seen, a very different, quite fantastic manner of getting Jesus' birth place being in Bethlehem. It is one with which we are very familiar, unfortunately so familiar that we don't see just how incredible it is! Luke's method is

6: O little town of Nazareth

to have the emperor Augustus call an otherwise unknown census. Of course, of such a massive undertaking as one calling for, 'the whole world to be enrolled' (Luke 2:1) we would expect to have been noted elsewhere in the records of antiquity. At the commencement of his gospel Luke seems keen to flout his historical credentials yet on this occasion he proves stunningly unsuccessful. We know that Augustus held a census of Roman citizens 8 BCE but no Roman census, however, would have been imposed on a client king such as Herod, and though not explicitly mentioned directly here Luke understands Herod the Great to be the ruler at the time of Jesus' birth. The empire was interested in only two things, the maintenance of the Pax Romana, the Roman peace, better understood by the modern catch-cry 'law and order,' and that the client state was paying its tribute to Rome. If the client ruler satisfied this two criteria Rome was happy. If Herod needed to ensure that sufficient taxes were being collected to satisfy both his needs and those of his patron and that this could be better done by ordering a census, then it would have been up to him to order such. Rome didn't have to micro-manage and had no interest in doing so. Such things they left to the client ruler and if Rome wasn't happy with that client they simply replaced them, usually by taking direct rule as was in the case, as seen, of two of Herod's sons, or by installing another client. It is possible that Augustus was behind the inauguration of a census taken every 14 years in Egypt of which we have records from 20 CE to 258 CE but that only serves to support what I have said for Rome was directly ruling Egypt during that period with the such practice occurring following the demise of the last Pharaoh, Queen Cleopatra.

Further the names, Augustus and Quirinius, along with their roles, Luke gives us as supposedly being contemporary with the calling of this census, don't mesh chronologically. While Augustus reigned over the whole period (27 BCE-14 CE), Herod died in 4 BCE while Quirinius did not become governor of Syria until 6-7 CE by which time Jesus was 10-11 years old. The inconsistencies with the dating were noted early and Tertullian (c.155-160- c. 220), one of the early church fathers, tried to solve the problem by 'correcting' the name of the Syrian governor, charging that it was Saturninus (9-6 BCE) rather than Quirinius who was the governor of Syria at the time of the census. Quirinius was the legate however in Syria during the time of the census so it has been argued that Luke mistakenly thought he was the already governor whereas his governorship came later. Josephus tells us that Quirinius did indeed call a census when he had assumed the governorship of Syria, and after Herod's successor, his son Archelaus, had been deposed by the Romans in favour of direct rule in Judea (Antiquities 17:13) Judea being a sub-district of Syria. This, Josephus tells us, was an unprecedented action with the goal being to assess property to register and of course tax it (Antiquities 18:1, 1-2). Once again this supports the argument that the Romans had no interest in such policy in a place under a client ruler but once they had taken direct control, as they now had in Judea, they no doubt wanted to collect information on the new province and so called a census. Elsewhere Luke tells us that this action led to a riot led by Judas the Galilean (Acts 5:37, c.f. Josephus Antiquities XXXVIII, 1). The date of that census however is too late to be associated with the birth of Jesus.

It should be noted that in calling this census Quirinius did so without calling on everyone to travel to their ancestral town. Forcing people to thus travel would be at total odds to the actual purpose of the census which was primarily for tax purposes, with taxation being levied on land locally owned. What purpose would be served then by then by making people leave the property they wished to assess and return to their ancestral homes? We can only ponder why would the Romans after calling a census to more efficiently collect revenue then go about doing so in a totally inefficient manner so antithetical to their aim? [2]

Luke, however, calls us to understand that the census required everyone to return to their home town. One can imagine the chaos that such a demand would cause even today with modern systems of transport! How much more then in times of primitive transport and rough roads? We are told that the holy family travelled to Bethlehem because Joseph was a descendant of King David. That may sound reasonable until we, as I earlier suggested, begin to guess at the numbers heading to Bethlehem remembering that King David had 300 wives. Given he died around 960 BCE one can scarcely imagine the number of descendants, that being made even worse when we are told his successor Solomon had 1,000 wives! We are told by Luke there were 42 generations between David and Joseph. How many descendants would David have had at that level of descent given that after 20 generations the average person monogamously married has approximately one million descendants? It certainly would have indeed been a good time in Bethlehem to be in the hospitality business! Little wonder Jesus' family, 'unable to find room in the inn' could only find rudimentary shelter.

Further these peoples' ability to trace their genealogical lines must have been highly impressive for we are to believe that, according to Luke's genealogy, they could do so over 42 generations. How many modern practitioners of the study of genealogy, with all the advantages at their disposal, would be able to match that?

We are next told that Joseph in response to the calling of the census makes his wife, 'heavily pregnant' travel with him walking or riding a donkey for 150 kilometres, about a week to ten days travel. There were of course remember, no hotels, motels or restaurants. Women were not counted in the census so why would he make her travel in such a state when she could have been left safely at home in the hands of relatives, many of them no doubt as women, better equipped than him to assist with the birth which could come at any time, even more so if one was undergoing such a gruelling journey. How much better a birth in familiar surroundings at home with help at hand rather than without help on the road? Mary has to come of course in order for Luke's theological schema of having Jesus born in Bethlehem, to be filled.

As with many of the Christmas stories this one has at its core a theological rationale. We find that again in how by calling this census Augustus Caesar inadvertently plays a significant role in the divine story. This parallels how long ago the Persian King Cyrus served as being the means of a great act of God, in such even being identified as 'Messiah' 'anointed one' (Isaiah 45:1), for his role in letting the captives in Babylon return to their homeland. Here, as with Cyrus, we have another leader of an empire, Caesar, with messianic pretensions, unknowingly playing a part in the divine story, by his calling of a census.

On arrival to Bethlehem Luke informs us that the birth of Jesus is in a manger for the inn was filled. From this it is assumed in the popular imagination that he was born in a stable as though a manger could not belong elsewhere. The manger however would not have been in a separate stable but rather a part of the house reserved for livestock. This was the case until comparatively recent times with the livestock being kept with the family within one enclosed space, usually on a lower level while the family lived on a raised dais. Most likely in such a case clean straw would have been used, perhaps in a manger brought up from downstairs to serve as a cradle. The stable so synonymous with the Christmas story belongs entirely to legend as likewise do the animals of popular imagination, not mentioned in the Scriptures, surrounding the manger. That cuts out a lot of Christmas cards! Having consigned the stable and animals to legend we can probably likewise dismiss the 'inn' for the term used by Luke 'kataluna' here translated 'inn' is better translated 'room.' When Luke wishes to speak of a commercial inn he uses the term 'pandocheion' as we find in his much beloved parable of the good Samaritan (Luke 10:34). The Last Supper on the other hand is held in a 'kataluna' or 'room' as the term there is correctly translated (Luke 22:11). Thus, there never was an 'inn' even more less one with 'no room.' The world of antiquity was not filled with hotel chains and the few inns that there were mostly were found only upon major roads, and that going to Bethlehem is unlikely to have been sufficiently important for such an establishment.

That Luke indicates of the 'inn' that there is 'no room' is most likely a metaphor used by him to indicate that by the time he was writing, many in Jesus' own nation had found no room in their hearts for him.

Of course, we get the inn and manger image from Luke's account whereas in Matthew's account we have the much less romantic place of Jesus' birth as being a 'house' (Matthew 2:11). Justin Martyr writing in the mid-2nd century informs us that the birthplace was a cave and that tradition was sufficiently strong for Constantine to build a church over what was believed to be the right cave c. 330 CE, which his later successor emperor, Justinian rebuilt in the 6th century. That place may still be visited in Bethlehem.

6: O little town of Nazareth

As A.N. Wilson bluntly comments of the Lukan birth narrative, 'it is a story which can still draw unbelievers to church once a year, and tears from their eyes as they behold the scene of the crib. But none of this delightful tableau is to be found in the pages of the New Testament.' [3]

Once Jesus is born Luke knowing nothing of the danger, which being all pervasive in Matthew's account forcing a desperate flight, instead has Jesus' parents stay with their infant in the place where Herod could have most easily found them, on his doorstep in Jerusalem, or in Bethlehem only a few kilometres distant. The parents remain in an open location carrying out in public all the rituals associated with the birth of a newborn.

The Mosaic Law provided for three ceremonies to follow the birth of a child (Leviticus 12, Exodus 13:1, 12, Numbers 18:15-16). The first rite had to do with the circumcision of the child on the eighth day, who then was usually also named, while the second rite concerned the price paid for the redemption of the first child and this could be done any time after the first month, while finally the third rite centred around the purification of the mother, who being 'unclean' because of childbirth was until that point disqualified from public worship. The Law prescribed that a woman was ritually unclean seven days after the birth of a son and 14 days after that of a daughter. Second, another level of uncleanliness was experienced for 33 days after the birth of a son and 66 after that of a daughter, after which a ceremony of dedication was carried out. Abhorrent as this sounds to modern ears we should remember that it was not long ago that a woman following childbirth would undergo 'churching' to be made clean again! Luke seems to confuse or conflate the second and third ceremonies, and it is for such mistakes that some scholars have judged him to be a gentile.

In Luke's gospel we find then that the family of Jesus assiduously carry out all required under the Law. Jesus is circumcised on the 8th day (Luke 2:21) as called for in the Torah (Leviticus 12:1-8) though here we are told 'after a week,' and presented and dedicated at the temple on the 40th day (Luke 2:22-24) in accord with that proscribed in the Law (Leviticus 12:6-8), although Luke seems to misunderstand it being

Jesus who needs purifying, where in actuality it is the mother, who bore the child, who must be purified.

That Jesus was so 'dedicated to the Lord' was required under the Mosaic Law whereby the first-born male was intended to be an offering to God and had therefore to be redeemed by another offering (Exodus 13:1, 11-16, Numbers 18:15-16). On this occasion, the family makes the requisite sacrifice called for by the Torah, their low economic status allowing them to choose the less expensive offering, two pigeons rather than a lamb and a pigeon. There are echoes in all this of course of a consecration, which in many cultures meant the literal sacrificing i.e. killing, of the first born as an offering to the Lord. This is what surely lies behind the story, where the idea of literally sacrificing the first child to the Lord is rejected of Abraham in the case of Isaac (Genesis 22:1-18). Such bloody practice is known from a range of religious traditions.

Luke, knowing nothing of Matthew's fear and danger, has then his story further continue in Jesus finding his place as one well settled within the Jewish tradition. Already the requisite rites have been completed and now two elders of that tradition cement his place within it. First we have the words of Simeon, a man 'righteous and devout' long looking for the 'consolation of Israel' who announces, in what has become known as the Nunc Dimittis (like the Magnificat from the opening words in Latin), his being able to 'depart in peace...for my eyes have seen the Lord's salvation which has been prepared in the presence of all peoples, the salvation which you have prepared for all peoples to see; a light to reveal your will to the gentiles' (Luke 2:25-32 c.f. Psalm 98, Isaiah 49:6). We may note again how Luke, while having Jesus firmly rooted in his own tradition, has also a strong universal theme that seen in the words, 'all peoples' and 'gentiles.' The words used here by Simeon are largely drawn from Isaiah 40-55 while the 'consolation of Israel' was the standard rabbinic description of the messianic age, an age where it was believed glory would come to Israel as all the nations of the world would stream to Zion. Luke however, has Simeon then add some words which hang heavy over the so far very comfortable story. Addressing Mary, he adds, 'Behold this child is set for the fall and rising of many in Israel, destined to be a sign that is spoken against, and a sword shall piece through your own soul and that the thoughts out of many hearts will be revealed' (Luke 2: 34-35). This again has a precedent in the tradition in the person of Isaiah (Isaiah 8:14-15).

Luke then follows with another holy person in Israel, a prophetess, Anna, acknowledging Jesus as being a very special part of the tradition in like manner to Simeon, seeing in him the redemption of Israel (Luke 2: 36-38). Such prophetesses were not unknown in the Hebrew Scriptures, examples being Deborah (Judges 4:4) and Huldah (2 Kings 22:14). Luke represents in many ways a feminine counterpart to Matthew. Thus, in Luke's gospel we find the revelation of the Messiah made to the women, Elizabeth and Mary, who affirm the good news they receive by the hymnic praise Luke places upon their lips, rather than to Matthew's Zechariah and Joseph. Further, on hearing from the believing women, Luke presents these two forenamed men as ones of doubt in contrast to the believing women. This emphasis on women fits with Luke's understanding that it is the poor and marginalised, the 'anawin' who have a central place in Jesus' ministry. Thus so, as we have just seen, he identifies the holy family as making the offering of the poor.

Further while Luke has those of questionable background, the shepherds, rather than Matthew's exotic wealthy wise men, as those who come to offer obeisance to the new born Messiah, they, though of questionable background, are still however within the tradition as distinct from Matthew, whose visitors must come from outside of that which he judges as the pernicious tradition. This again fits both authors' schemas, Matthew's rejection and enmity of the ongoing Jewish tradition in relation to the Jesus movement, and Luke having Jesus sit comfortably within Judaism just as the faith which he spawns, Christianity, sits comfortably with Rome as a respectable faith. If Matthew wants to speak of the new wine not being able to be contained within old wine skins Luke would wish to assert that there is no need to so totally juxtapose the message of Jesus against its surrounding milieu with perhaps a grafting of the vine better suiting his schema.

After spending all this time at peace in Jerusalem where Luke has them welcomed into and finding peace in the tradition the holy family then peacefully return to their home town in Galilee (Luke 2:39).

This is a far cry as we have seen from Matthew's account where the danger is so great the holy family following the birth of Jesus must immediately flee, with that danger, now coming from Herod's son Archelaus, still being present even after several years exile in Egypt, again precluding the family, on their return from Egypt, from staying in Jerusalem or its surrounds and needing therefore to travel north to Nazareth.

Perhaps we are shocked to find that Jesus almost certainly was not born in the holy town of Bethlehem, for don't we sing about this 'fact' so often in our Christmas carols, but rather in Nazareth. There were, as we have seen, strong theological reasons for having Jesus born in Bethlehem as that was from where everybody in the Jewish tradition knew the Messiah must come and so in attempting to prove that Jesus, despite all contrary appearances, is the Messiah both Matthew and Luke appropriate the messianic Bethlehem tradition. Elsewhere however it is simply assumed that Jesus is a Nazarene with John of course, as earlier noted, letting the cat out of the bag by specifically stating that indeed Nazareth was the place of his birth.

Yet I believe theologically there is something profound in having Jesus as Messiah come from Nazareth. That birthplace is another indicator of from which side of history the divine wishes to be present. Jesus is not born in the auspicious place from where it was widely expected that the Messiah would come but rather is born in a place not even mentioned in the sacred tradition, in that part of the land, Galilee, which the religious establishment, centred in Judea, regarded as being of questionable piety. As was Jesus born in scandal to an unwed mother to an unknown father, so too was he born into that place from 'which nothing good can come.' God chooses to be made present on the underside, the neglected side of history. We could put it colloquially as a bastard child born in a bastard place? Seen from this underside the nativity story begins to take on a whole new, and for me, more profound meaning.

Endnotes

1 The parallel is of course that Jesus, as representative of a new Israel, spends 40 days in the desert successfully overcoming temptation while the old Israel succumbs to temptation

during its 40-year pilgrimage in that same domain. Jesus then goes to be baptized by John in the Jordan. He goes under the water thereby parting it, just as the Israel of old entered the 'promised land' under Joshua, through the parting of the Jordan. The Sermon on the Mount as a new Law 'you have heard it said…. but I say to you', parallels the reception of the Law by Moses on Mount Sinai or Horeb. This is all of course classic use of midrash.

2 It must be said, however, that C. Vibius Maximus, a prefect of Rome in 104CE tells us of just such a practice in Egypt carried out in a provincial census 'Seeing that the time has come for a house to house census, it is necessary to compel all those for any cause whatsoever are residing out of their provinces to return to their own homes, that they may both carry out the regular order of the census and may attend diligently to the cultivation of their allotments. This however seems to refer only to those who are on holidays or even extended leave of absence. It does not have any reference to returning to some ancestral home in which one may not have lived for hundreds of years.

3 A.N. Wilson: Jesus, Flamingo, London,1993:80

7: Massacre at Bethlehem

Part of the 'known' Christmas story is the 'massacre of the innocents' carried out by Herod's forces, still commemorated in the church calendar usually three days after Christmas as 'the massacre of the innocents.' As we have seen the account only features in Matthew's gospel following Joseph's dream warning Jesus' parents to flee Bethlehem before the planned massacre took place. We have noted on the other hand how on the contrary Luke has the family with newborn living in blissful peace in the same locale.

Although we only move forward a few days in the church's liturgical calendar, we could be moving forward for maybe up to two years given that King Herod having become the Pharaoh like figure of evil authority feels the need to kill all male children under that age in the area in his attempt to kill this king/messiah pretender. Probably, however the event is probably meant to be one taking place just following the birth of the one it was designed to eliminate. What we know of Herod the Great would show that such was not beyond him, for even his favourite wife and children were not spared his paranoia around holding power. The Emperor Octavius was alleged to say that he would prefer to be Herod's pig than his family. Herod was evidently sufficiently pious, at least publicly, as a 'Jew' according to Octavius, to make the choice of being his pig a safer one than to be a family member!

One of the Idumeans, who had been forcibly converted to Judaism by John Hyracanus around 130-120 BCE, Herod had a fearsome reputation but was also a wily leader. As a shrewd politician Herod had skilfully curried favour with successive competing Roman parties across all the many political power plays in the empire during this time. Thus so, he first was able to win the favour of Pompey, who had conquered the Holy Land in 63 BCE. Later, despite his earlier support of Pompey he was still able to gain the trust of Pompey's conqueror Julius Caesar, before again winning the favour of Caesar's assassin Cassius, and then in turn Caesar's avenger Mark Antony, before finally coming out of the

Roman civil war on the winning side of Octavius (Augustus). Quite the scheming political broker!

That political skill had enabled Herod's rise to power following a dispute among the Hasmoneans. With the High Priesthood in their family the Hasmoneans had ruled the Holy Land, but an argument broke out between Hyrcanus and his brother Antigonus, the result being that Antigonus successfully usurped the High Priesthood. This division gave the shrewd operator Herod his chance and on approaching the Romans he was declared king by Antony and Octavius in 40 BCE though he did not claim his throne until 37 BCE.

Herod was a tyrannical ruler and his cruel actions within even his own family are legendary but being a mere despotic tyrant did not however guarantee success in the Roman Empire. Indeed, it could bring one's downfall in that it could lead to a popular uprising, which would disturb the order so admired by the Romans, who to restore 'peace', the 'pax Romana,' may well depose the tyrant, either by replacing him with another member of the local royalty or by simply taking direct control, the latter being the fate of two of Herod's sons as we shall further examine. That Herod ruled for a long time shows that he was no mere tyrannical despot but rather an astute leader obviously satisfying the Romans as to both his competency and his ability to keep his subjects largely content, and when needed, under control. Within the empire this was how an effective ruler ruled, skilfully adjusting the levers between keeping the populace content and cracking down when needed. Herod probably tended to the style of rule by terror but was obviously sufficiently astute to know when to ease back and keep the populace happy. A show of piety could go a long way to doing that, and there could be no greater show of piety than the massive Temple, one of the masterpieces of the ancient world, which Herod had re-built on an almost unimaginable scale.

Herod lived a dissolute lifestyle, having we are told ten wives, while killing any of his children whom he regarded as threats to his throne. On coming to power Josephus tells us that in one of his first acts he massacred 45 leading men of Israel for resisting his occupation of Jerusalem. But Herod as we have just seen also knew how to appeal to

7: Massacre at Bethlehem

his subjects. As well as building the Temple he further demonstrated his supposed piety by reinstituting the High Priesthood, bringing back the over-thrown Hyrcanus, but with the office of course being stripped of power and made strictly a-political. Despite those precautions Hyrcanus still proved too popular so Herod resorted to his usual recourse and had him executed.

Of course, not being Jewish but rather an Idumean, there were always questions as to Herod's legitimacy as a Jewish king. To satisfy such questioning, as well as re-building the temple and re-instituting the High Priesthood, Herod sought to secure legitimacy in Jewish eyes by his marriage to Mariamne, of the legitimate Hasmonean line. She of course, being of that line, represented however a threat to his power and so in turn she met her grisly demise at her husband's hand. So disconsolate however was Herod at her death he was said to have kept her body, which he regularly viewed, preserved in a large tub of honey. Such sentimentality of love however could not be allowed to interfere with this ruthless man's securing an ever-stronger hold on power by his removal of any perceived threat, real or otherwise. For like reason five sons, as noted, met death at his hand, two he had by Mariamne, along with another he had by his first wife Doris while yet still another two met like fate. Little wonder then Octavius' aforesaid comment!

As well as building to satisfy attempts at Jewish piety, Herod also built structures which showed his cosmopolitan Hellenistic interests, constructing those two paradigms of Greek culture, a theatre and a stadium in Jerusalem, these, of course, not going down so well with those of his subjects who were pious. He was not only a benefactor in Israel but also sponsored public works in Greece, including subsidizing the restoration of a Temple to Apollo on Rhodes and even sponsoring the Olympics. Such a building programme secured him a good reputation and patronage in the wider Roman world and as we have seen Herod liked to play well to all those who would facilitate his holding power and in that he was wildly successful.

Herod's reign was as long as it was cruel with Josephus telling us he reigned 37 years from the official date of his been given the throne by Octavian and Antony in 40 BCE while mentioning that just before his death there was an eclipse of the moon (Antiquities 17:167). As this is the only time Josephus mentions this type of celestial phenomena it is unlikely to be fabricated and we know that there was such an eclipse 12-13 March 4 BCE. We also learn from Josephus that Passover followed soon after the tyrant's death (Antiquities 17:213, Jewish War 2:10), and given that year Passover was celebrated 11 April we can narrow down to a matter of weeks the time of Herod's demise. That death was of a particularly gruesome manner, a gangrenous flesh disease of unceasing pain, fit for such a tyrant. Of course, with the Jewish aversion to any disease of the flesh such as leprosy this was particularly galling, with many of course seeing this as a divine judgement being played out on the tyrant. Josephus tells us, almost certainly with more than a touch of hyperbole, that Herod had ordered a member of every family be killed at the time of his death so to ensure that there would be mourning across the land. The reality was that with the iron fist now gone popular rebellion broke out. [1]

By the time of his death Herod had fallen out, due to his invasion of Nabatea, with his Roman patron Augustus, who consequently refused to ratify Herod's will in which he had left his kingdom to Archelaus. Augustus ruled instead that Herod's kingdom be divided three ways between his sons, with Archelaus receiving Judea, Samaria and Idumea, Antipas (the Herod referred to during Jesus' ministry) receiving Galilee and Perea while a half-brother Philip received parts of southern Syria. None were permitted to carry the esteemed title 'king' but rather were to rule by the lesser titles tetrarch and 'ethnarch.' Archelaus' rule was so tyrannical, fermenting such resistance from his subjects that the Romans, so to preserve 'the peace,' deposed him in 6 CE taking direct control of his kingdom through prefects and procurators, the best known of course being Pontius Pilate. Philip would rule for some 40 years but he too was finally removed by the Romans for an act of hubris whereby, on the urgings of his wife we are told, he had asked to be made 'king.' Antipas following accusation by his nephew Agrippa I of his being involved in a conspiracy against the new emperor, Caligula would end up being exiled to Gaul in 39 CE on that emperor's orders.

7: Massacre at Bethlehem

Though from the aforesaid it would seem Herod was capable of such a massacre as that of 'the innocents' there is no record of such, save in Matthew's gospel although it has been argued that possibly 'only' twenty of that age would have been living in that area meaning it wouldn't make the front-page memory for many contemporary writers. There is perhaps an echo of such a massacre in Jewish legend of that time which was later taken up into the haggadah (a story illustrative of a section of the Torah) read at Passover. [2] In that story Pharaoh was warned that the infant Moses would usurp the throne unless he was killed, but the story tells us that Moses had been saved by the angel Gabriel. There may be a reflection in this haggadah of a real event to do with Herod or perhaps conversely, and I believe more likely, it is from this haggadah concerning Moses that this story of Herod's massacre finds its genesis. Like Moses, Jesus is saved from Herod's vengeance with salvation coming again through the intervention of an angel, this time in a warning given to Joseph to flee. From the non-Jewish tradition, we have a similar story with the Roman historian Suetonius telling us that shortly before the emperor Octavius was born an omen suggested that another who would become the ruler of Rome had been born, leading the republican Senate to decree that all males born that year should die. Of course, this extreme story like that in the Scriptures is legendary. Given the divisions in Rome at the time of the birth of Octavius it is highly unlikely that the Senate would have been sufficiently united to have decreed such, and clearly this story operated as propaganda designed to bolster Octavius' somewhat, at that stage, shaky hold on the throne.

There was no massacre of the infants by Herod. It is inconceivable to think that Herod, being the tyrant he was with powerful backers, felt threatened in any way by an insignificant infant peasant child, nor as an astute political player would he be likely to commit such an act which in its sheer cruelty would have bred rebellion when simply there was no need to do such. This story rather is another case of midrash connecting the birth of Jesus with that of Moses, that connection, as we have seen, being so important for Matthew. Indeed, not only in the infancy narrative but right through his gospel, as we have found,

Matthew is keen to make that Moses connection. Thus, so here the birth of Jesus like that of Moses, is surrounded by danger fermented at the hands of a tyrant with both Moses and Jesus, their lives endangered, being forced to flee as refugees, Moses from Egypt to the Promised land, Israel, though he himself would never arrive there, and Jesus carried by his family in that reverse exodus from Israel to Egypt. This flight as such has then no historical reality but rather represents a theological construction developed by Matthew out of his negative view of the ongoing mainline Jewish tradition against which he was fighting. As we have seen the followers of Jesus, though they wished in the main, at least in the Matthean church, to remain as faithful Jews were increasingly being rejected by the establishment in this new style of Judaism set upon of course establishing itself, and were being forced to exit (make an exodus) from their tradition. The journey into Egypt, necessary to escape the wrathful Jewish authorities, even though that wrathful role must be played by Herod, hardly a paragon of Jewish piety but still the Jewish king, reflects that antipathy and separation of the followers of Jesus from their contemporary Judaism. It is this theological, rather than historical reality, which both serves to create and shape the telling of the story of the holy family needing to go into exile. The Matthean Jesus' exodus reflects then the increasingly forced exodus of the 'Jesus Jews' from their faith tradition rather than any historical reality.

Thus again, as in all these Christmas narratives, we have a story shaped by theology rather than history. In this case the theology which shapes the story is that of Matthew wanting to affirm that it is his small band of 'Jesus Jews,' rather than that mainstream Judaism re-organising under Johannan ben Zakkai, who represent the true inheritors of the sacred tradition. In such an instance, one naturally paints their opponents most darkly as does Matthew not only in this nativity story but indeed right through his account. Though Matthew and his community believe they are the true inheritors of the Jewish tradition it is they themselves who are being forced more and more into exile from the re-organising Judaism, and it is that forced exile which serves as the basis for this story. That the exile in this story is to Egypt, the epitome of oppression

7: Massacre at Bethlehem

in the Jewish mind, only serves to heighten the charge which Matthew is making concerning his Jewish opponents. This fleeing to the gentile land is a symbol of the gospel mantle, given the rejection of most of the Jews, being now in Matthew's understanding, handed over to the gentiles. Just after the furore he causes at the Temple with his turning over of the money-changers' tables, and shortly before his arrest, Matthew has Jesus tell a whole series of parables making this point (Matthew 21:12:19, 28-43) culminating in the line, 'I tell you then, that the kingdom of God will be taken from you and given to a people who will produce its fruit.' We sadly know that such statements have had a long and dark providence in the history of how Christians have viewed the Jewish people with the most horrific results. It is good to remind ourselves that when Matthew has Jesus make such statements that both he and his Jesus speak such words out of powerlessness, and do so also as Jews. This is far different to how such stories, in gentile hands have been (mis)appropriated in the long and dark history of anti-Semitism.

There is an attractiveness in this story of Jesus and his family being forced on to the road as refugees because of tyrannical violent exercise of power. The story shows just to what length a tyrant, ancient or modern, will go to preserve their power against threat. In a world faced with refugee numbers as never seen before in history (some 60 million at the time of writing), that being a result of tyrannical rule in so many places, and an increasing resistance to both their plight and flight, especially as earlier noted in my country, there is something most appealing about having Jesus identified as being one of them, forced onto the road in desperate escape. As a refugee, his family fleeing for their lives from a wrathful, even megalomaniacal, tyrant Jesus is identified with the underside of history. Thus, while the flight of the Joseph, Mary and child has no historical basis there are still clear theological lessons to be drawn from it which call us to another way of acting in face of the major refugee crisis in our world today. As such the story, while not having a factual basis, contains within it, along with as we have noted, many of the nativity episodes, a profound truth. Again, we find the truth of the Christmas narratives not in their factuality but in another place, a deeper place, which is I contend where the authors intended us to look.

Endnotes

1 Following the time of Herod the Great's death and the turmoil it unleashed there were numerous rebellions led by such figures as Judas in Galilee, Simon in Perea and Athronges in Judea. No Roman legions were stationed in the Jewish state but due to the turmoil following Herod's death three legions were sent south by the governor of Syria Publius Quinctilius Varus to quell these rebellions. Two thousand insurrectionists were crucified outside Jerusalem.

2 The Haggadah is a legend, parable or anecdote used to illustrate a point of the Law. More specifically it relates to the telling of the Passover story in Passover celebration.

8: The Heavenly portents tell?

It hardly need be said that stories of stars moving sufficiently slow as to be able to be followed, reversing direction and then stopping over a particular house are surely not the things of history but rather of mythology! Relative to the earth a star at the equator moves at some 1,650 kilometres per hour so that certainly was some pace these wise men kept up over a substantial time. An Olympic marathon runner would have nothing but envy for them, and this all done drug free! Then having been westward proceeding to bring the wise men to Jerusalem the star stops over that city while the they meet with Herod, before turning then to move in the contrary direction to Bethlehem, before again stopping in that place right over the house they seek as though close enough to signal out a particular home.

Such an event only makes sense of course in an age that had a primitive minuscule cosmology, where the sky was understood to be a vault from which God could hang out a lantern at important moments. Our modern cosmological knowledge makes such exceedingly quaint. With our current state of knowledge, we estimate that there are perhaps 200 billion stars just in our galaxy and that there are some 200 billion other galaxies beside ours. It is good to stop here and take a moment to consider those numbers by again reading and pondering them rather than just glossing over them. In our galaxy alone, there are sufficient stars for each person of earth to possess around 29 of them and that's just our galaxy! In the universe, there are billions of stars for each of us along with numerous galaxies! Utterly amazing isn't it? So much more so than the quaint biblical astronomy. I know my mind gets totally blown each time I think on it. These hundreds of billions of stars, all impersonal physical objects moving away from us at phenomenal rates, are mostly massive and of course obviously not subject to any events upon our minuscule earth, incredibly remote from them. They all have a fixed trajectory and any past or future location of each relative to us can be calculated and charted exactly. It goes without saying then that none of them wander even reversing direction. This of all stories within the nativity narratives is certainly no story to be taken literally! Clearly the object sighted and followed was not a star. Could it have been some other celestial object?

There has been much speculation as to the nature of 'the star.' John Kepler in 1603, observing the conjunction of Saturn and Jupiter in the constellation of Pisces, calculated that there had been a very similar occurrence in 7 BCE. He was even able to find a rabbinical reference in the Aggadoth Mashiach asserting that the Messiah would come when there was a conjunction of Jupiter and Saturn in the constellation of Pisces. However, the conjunction of that time doesn't appear to have been close enough so as appear to be a single 'star.' He also speculated that the magi may have witnessed a birth of a new star, what we know now as a supernova. A supernova was observed and recorded by the Chinese Han dynasty for 70 days in 5 BCE. But as we have seen the contrary movement precludes a star. Edmund Halley calculated that the comet, named after him following its passing of the earth in 1682, had also similarly passed the earth in 12 BCE. This however is too early for the birth of Jesus. Modern astronomers inform us that there was a conjunction of Venus and Jupiter 12 August 3 BCE. If there is an historical basis for the event the obvious occurrence would have been a conjunction of planets as only this would allow for the necessary retrograde movement west to east, for planets relative to the stars, will on occasions appear to move thus due to their orbits being further from the sun than that of the earth. Probably some residual memory of a recent comet or most likely a conjunction of planets lies behind the story and that event then became linked to the birth of Jesus with the details of the astronomical event being exaggerated over time and turned to legend. What is important is not the specifics of the actual event but rather the knowledge that in the ancient world a celestial event was often understood as being the prerequisite for the birth of such a prominent figure as Matthew believed Jesus to be. Making this point is Matthew's aim and that is why he makes use of an astronomical phenomena, perhaps by co-opting a residual memory of one or a combination of astrological events, and applying them to the birth of Jesus.

8: The Heavenly portents tell?

Again, this story appears to be another example of midrash with Matthew possibly having in mind the idea behind such a text as, 'a star shall come out of Jacob' (Numbers 24:17). There the one speaking of the star, Balaam, is another seer from the East, associated with sighting a star, as were the wise men, (Numbers 23:7, 24:3-4, 15-17). While Matthew doesn't quote this text, it does appear in the messianic texts from the Qumran community (Community Document vii:19, Teacher of Righteousness and Testament of Levi 18:3). A later Jewish revolt, some 100 years after the time of Jesus (132-135 CE) against Roman rule would be led by a Simon bar Kosiba called 'bar Kokhba' (son of a star). The star association, which he cleverly used, had messianic implications and many of his followers regarded bar Kokhba as the Messiah.

Matthew's intention is to inform us is that the birth of Jesus is so significant that even the heavens must tell of it. Luke in his infancy narrative, as we shall see, for like reason, will replace the light of the star with another heavenly light, that of heavenly figures and an angelic chorus.

As to the men who follow the star we are again, as in so much of the Christmas story, in the realm of midrash. We get the figures of the magi from the east from Isaiah 60, where already they are kings, that of course helping to explain the later elevation in the tradition of Matthew's wise men to likewise being kings. There we are also told they come from Sheba bringing with them gold and frankincense, that leaving us with the need to get myrrh into the story as the third gift. The myrrh connection is again with Sheba for that place in Isaiah's story would have reminded Matthew of another story naming Sheba as the locale, from where another royal visitor came to pay homage to an earlier 'king of the Jews.' That visitor from was no less than the queen of that place, from which she came to pay homage to Solomon (I Kings 1: 10-13). The Queen of Sheba like the magi came on camels laden with spice, with myrrh being no doubt understood by Matthew to be among those spices. Each of the gifts named has a link to the Hebrew Scriptures; gold (Psalm 72:15), frankincense (Isaiah 60:6) and myrrh (Psalm 45:8, Song of Songs 3:6). Probably Matthew also adds the myrrh as an indication of what he knows will finally become of his newborn, myrrh being associated with burial. The gifts serve as a further reason for the three visitors to be later in the second century elevated to become kings, for it is kings who bring such gifts and offer obeisance to the Messiah (Psalm 72:10, Isaiah 49:7, 60: 3-10). Elsewhere it was said that such figures, the three sons of Parthian rulers, came with the Armenian king. Tiridates to pay homage to Nero as god at Naples in 66CE. Tiridates was also a Zoroastrian priest. This is only some two decades before Matthew writes so he may have had this event in mind when he has such homage being paid to the one he understands as both king and divine.

Who are these wise men who follow the star? Again, we need to remind ourselves again that in the Matthean account they were not kings and further that there were not even necessarily three of them. It is only later in the Christian tradition that these wise men or magi are turned into kings, both under the influence of the above referred Scriptures but also to make the point that even the kings of this earth come to pay obeisance to this king, king over all kings. If this infant is the one being described by the early church as both being superior and also standing in opposition to the kings of the world, as king of kings, what better way to show this than to have kings come and offer obeisance to him? This was even more the case following the Empire becoming Christianised from the time of Constantine, after which Jesus in description and image comes to bear all the marks of being a king; crowned, enthroned and holding a sceptre. While earlier he was king as a critique of the kings of this world, he then however became one, who as a supreme king served to justify all kings and their rule.

The wise men we are told bear three gifts; frankincense, myrrh and gold. That of course does not necessarily logically mean there were three men bearing the three gifts as though each held one gift with Matthew himself giving us no number as to the wise men. If we dig back into the Hebrew Scriptures we will again find from where the number three was derived (Psalm 72: 10). There of David we read of three kings bringing gifts, 'May the kings of Tarshish and of distant shores bring tribute to him. May the kings of Sheba and Seba present him gifts.' Again, we find at play here Matthew's schema of linking Jesus to King David.

8: The Heavenly portents tell?

As we know the wise men are also called magi. The term 'magi' is the plural of the term 'magus' (Latin) and goes back to the term 'magos' (Greek) meaning one who is a magician or a sorcerer, or one adept at reading astrological signs and dreams. To the east in Persia, from where it is likely they came, such things were associated with the priestly caste and Herodotus (c.484-430-420 BCE) had long before intrigued his Greek readers by his description of them. The assumption is nearly always made that they were gentiles but there were well established extensive Jewish communities living in the east, having remained resident in those places when others had returned to Israel after the Babylonian exile which had ended 522-521 BCE, so it is possible the sojourners were Jewish. Indeed, several large Jewish communities remained in the east up to recent times. Thus, so the Babylonian or Bavli Talmud would be of greater in importance than that emanating out of Jerusalem.

On arriving at Jerusalem as we know the wise men seek directions as to the birthplace of the Messiah. Herod would have most likely taken an interest in astronomy as Jewish interest in that subject is well attested, a work from that time, the 'Treatise of Shemi' showing that even among the Qumran literature horoscopes have been found. If found among a group so strongly rejecting outside culture that they had fled to the desert, it is highly likely that astronomy was widely practiced within Judaism. Such use of the heavens to make predictions of coming kings is also found in Josephus who tells of an Egyptian scholar who thus predicted the coming of a Pharaoh (Antiquities ii: 205-206, 215).

In summary this story as we have seen was clearly lifted from the realm of myth where such celestial events are associated with the births of the great, while from within Judaism the midrash connections with another eastern seer, Balaam are clear. Further from within that same Jewish tradition the star had messianic connotations, that being most clearly seen in the Bar Kockba episode.

Again, in line with Matthew's theological project Herod, the Jewish king is portrayed as an evil figure while the pagan (though as we have seen they may have been Jewish but in any case, coming from outside the Jerusalem establishment) wise men are portrayed in a positive light.

Unlike Herod who uses even the Scriptures as a means of planning his evil, the magi seemingly without the advantage of these, make use of the pagan means of astrology and unlike Herod in their search for the child do so with a pure motive. The contrast drawn by Matthew between the two parties could hardly be clearer.

Again, with this story it is a pity to strip away the factual historical nature which as we have seen is frankly unbelievable, for theologically there is much in this account. In a world where the Christian faith has been so totally co-opted by the established order there is something powerfully attractive in this story in which a person like Herod understands the threat of the true Christian message to the way of being and power as represented by him. We are challenged to understand the radical nature of the kingdom this king brings and to resist such co-option to the rule of the Herods of this world. That the rulers of the world are seen in this story to pay homage to one who rules in a way totally contrary to power as commonly exercised is evidence of the true power of a gospel, free from such co-option by the powers of this world. It stands rather above and in judgment of them.

Though they do it in different ways, both Matthew and Luke want to associate this birth of the Messiah with heavenly portents and with visitors who come to see the divine one in response to those portents. This is, as we have found, totally appropriate as messianic figures in the ancient world often had births associated with such heavenly events. For Matthew, the birth is marked by the star westward, then eastward proceeding, followed by the wise men or magi while for Luke it is a humbler set of visitors, the shepherds who come to pay homage, following their being recipients of a heavenly vision.

Let us turn now to the Lukan story with its different heavenly portents. As noted earlier it would be highly unlikely that shepherds would be in the fields with their flocks in the dead of winter in December when overnight temperatures drop near to or below zero. Still the December date is one arrived at well after the biblical period. It was, as seen, a means of co-opting the Roman feast of Saturnalia, a celebration of the passing of the winter solstice and the increasing return of the invincible sun. The usual actual practice with livestock was to place the sheep in the fields after the June wheat harvest to graze on the remains. Thus, if there is any historical kernel to this story then it seems Jesus was born in the northern summer, rather than in the depths of winter as would be the case with a December birth-date.

In the Lukan account, the shepherds in the field initially see an angel of the Lord with glory shining all around them. Once again of course we are with the Jewish shekinah. This of course is a typical type of epiphany found across all sorts of spiritual traditions, including that of the Jews, but it still startling enough to invoke fear in the shepherds. The angel, after telling them not to fear, then goes on to inform them that, 'this day in the town of David, a saviour has been born to you; he is Christ the Lord' before then informing them of the specifics of how this one will appear, 'a baby wrapped in swaddling clothes and lying in a manger.' If the shepherds' trepidation had calmed somewhat it must have again been raised by the then sudden appearance of, 'a great throng of heavenly hosts' singing the praises of this event which brings 'glory to God and peace on earth.' Having been informed of this great happening the shepherds decide to make a visit, where they tell the no doubt incredulous family of all the things which had happened to them.

Having made that visit the shepherds return singing praises to God and offering the good news to any who would listen. In accord with Luke's theology there is a strong universal component in the message the shepherds give. Thus, the coming saviour brings peace to all the earth and good will to all. The term used to describe the role of Jesus, 'saviour' is common in pagan religions as earlier noted, and is far less exclusive than the specific Jewish term, 'Messiah' used in Matthew's gospel. Of the shepherd's visit Mary is left to contemplate all these things treasuring their memory (Luke 2:19).

Shepherds lay at the margins of Jewish respectability. Though the trade was not technically one which was impure it certainly was questionable. Who after all could know the level of adherence to all the ritual codes by such figures out in the hills, especially when they are resident, as I take them to be given Jesus' real birthplace, in already dubious Galilee? There are rabbinic writings which speak of neglectful nature of shepherd's observance of the Torah (Shek vii:4,

Baba K vii:7, 80a). Yet the figure of the shepherd is also ambiguous for had not Israel's greatest king, David been a shepherd (I Samuel 16-17)? The locale in which David practiced his occupation was of course Bethlehem. The Messiah was expected out of David's line, so it makes sense to have those of David's profession, supposedly residing in Bethlehem, recognise the Messiah come among them. Jesus himself would be understood in the Christian tradition as both shepherd (John 10:1-18) and lamb (John 1:29, 36). From the pagan tradition, this idyllic tale echoes the presence of shepherds at the births of famous figures, most notably Romulus and Remus.

The angelic song associated with the celestial display could be a means used by Luke to suggest that in the birth of this child there is nothing less than a new creation, for at the commencement of creation itself from the Hebrew Scriptures we read, 'the morning stars sang together' (Job 38:7). This type of overwhelming epiphany is not of course unknown in the Hebrew Scriptures where, as here, it understandably invokes fear, examples including; Moses standing before the burning bush (Exodus 3:1-4), the pillar of cloud and fire in the desert during the exodus (Exodus 13:21-22) and again Moses only being allowed to see the rear end of God in a cleft in the rock (Exodus 33:20-23) and finally Isaiah's terrifying vision at his commissioning (Isaiah 1). In the synoptic gospel tradition, we have in like manner the Transfiguration, where Jesus, along with Peter, John and James, ascends a mountain whereupon the four of them experience a truly awesome revelation which brings great fear upon the three disciples (Mark 9:2-8 and pars).

The words 'good news' and 'saviour' used in this story echo some inscriptions found in Asia Minor, commemorating the birth of another divine messiah come to bring peace to the world, Augustus. By using the ascription, 'saviour' normally only ascribed to Augustus and his successors, and Augustus uses it of himself when he boasts in his autobiographical 'Res Gestae,' Luke is doing something quite seditious by applying it to Jesus. It is largely not known that all those words we believe originated with the Christian description of Jesus have their basis in their use by the Roman Empire. Caesar was 'saviour' and 'Lord' and thus worthy of worship as the 'son of God' one who being 'divine,'

8: The Heavenly portents tell?

had brought 'peace' (the Pax Romana) to the world. The gospel usage is a radical co-option, and therefore dangerous claim, on these things properly belonging to Caesar, attributing them then to another, one shamefully executed no less, in the face of Roman power.

It is of course not important that Matthew's westward proceeding 'star' followed by the wise men ever existed or that Luke's great heavenly portent of the angelic chorus had any real existence. What is crucial is that which both gospel writers are suggesting in their use of the common myth of heavenly portents, these being associated with great rulers holding divine attributes. By such link both are claiming that in this vulnerable peasant child, born in a place of no honour, in a manner which attracted scandalous comment, there has come one has who ranks with, indeed above, the kings and great figures of the world! His 'rule' however will be of an entirely different manner to that exercised by these other rulers and as such represents a direct critique and challenge to their style. The response to this subversive challenge is therefore Herod's action, his massacre of the infants, a precursor to that action later carried out by the Empire against this one who dared claim to be a king. Both evangelists challenge us as to which ruler will we follow and in who's kingdom do we wish to reside? Are we entranced by the great signs of power and prestige associated with the kingdoms of this world, or are we open to a different epiphany? The history may not be real; the theological and ethical challenge however is very much so.

9: Who is the Greatest?

Immediately apparent on reading Luke's infancy narrative is that it contains not one but two birth narratives, that of John the Baptist as well as that of Jesus. Luke gives us the two narratives because he wishes to connect the two births right from conception through to birth and then on into their lives and shared violent executions as though the two figures essentially belong together, John of course being subject to Jesus. That almost was, especially when it comes to their adult lives, certainly not the case. Elsewhere, as we shall see, though they had many commonalities, there actually was a degree of antipathy between the two grown figures. John certainly was not, as presented in Luke, a second in charge subservient to Jesus being then superseded by him. The connection between John and Jesus is so important for Luke that he presents them as cousins. That they are cousins enables Luke to further reinforce the subservience of John for it is he, the older cousin, who will be subservient to the younger.

Luke establishes this relationship between John and Jesus by the numerous commonalities he gives in their births? Indeed, by giving us so many parallels it is clear Luke doesn't want us to miss that point. First, the angel Gabriel announces the coming births of each (Luke 1:13, 1:31) with both the recipients, Zechariah and Mary being troubled by the angel's appearance (Luke 1:12, 1:29), meaning that the angel must reassure each of them (Luke 1:13, 1:30-31). Next the future destiny of both John and Jesus is given by the angel's use of exalted poetic language (Luke1:14-17, 1:32-33), with both recipients then querying their angelic herald (Luke 1:18, 1:34) with the result being that each is given a sign, Zechariah being struck dumb (Luke 1:20) while Mary is told of Elizabeth's pregnancy (Luke 1:36). We are then told of both John and Jesus that they were each named unconventionally and of course, as we would expect, that they were both circumcised (Luke 1:59-63, 2:21). Finally, we are informed how all the events surrounding both births led to amazement (Luke 1:65-66, 2:17-18) being then blessed by the utterance of a prophetic poem (Luke 1:67-79, 2:28-32). Though there are similarities in kind there are very deliberately differences in degree, the latter indicating which of Jesus and John shall take precedence, with that precedence in Luke's eyes clearly belonging to Jesus.

Having established the connections let us now examine those differences in degree. First, we find the angel Gabriel saying of John 'he will be great before the Lord' (Luke 1:15), but of Jesus 'he will be great, and will be called Son of the Most High' (Luke 1:32). When John is born only 'neighbours and relatives' rejoice (Luke 1:58) while Jesus' birth brings 'a multitude of the heavenly host praising God' (Luke 2:13). The public presentation and prophecy of destiny for each child finds John presented in his parents' home with reports going merely to the neighbours and the surrounding hill country (Luke 1:65-79) while Jesus is presented not in the home but rather in the Temple, with the report going out to all 'who were looking for the redemption of Jerusalem' that of course implying everybody (Luke 2:21-38). In their maturation while John grows 'strong in spirit' (Luke 1:80) Jesus grows 'filled with the wisdom, and the favour of God was upon him... [so that] Jesus increased in wisdom and stature, and in favour of God and people' (Luke 2:40-52). Finally, while John's character is developing hidden in the wilderness (Luke 1:80) Jesus was already astonishing the teachers in the Temple at age twelve (Luke 2:41-50). The subservience of John to Jesus in this gospel is most clearly seen of course in the episode before either of their births when Mary visits her older cousin Elizabeth. On that occasion Mary's greeting causes the child in Elizabeth's womb to 'leap for joy' (Luke 1:41). Even while they are still in the womb we are clearly meant to understand John's subservience to his younger 'cousin.'

In Luke's account the story of the birth of John the Baptist clearly represents but a prelude to the more spectacular and more important event, the birth of Jesus. Let's first turn to examine the prelude concerning John, in a sense only important for what it foreshadows, before then examining John's actual relationship with Jesus.

On turning to the infancy narrative concerning the Baptist we first read of how Zechariah, John's father, a priest of the line of Abijah, has the greatest honour, a once in a lifetime opportunity to bring the

9: Who is the greatest?

incense offertory.[1] On entering the temple to burn the incense he receives a revelation, given by Gabriel, one of the seven archangels of Jewish tradition, that he and his wife Elizabeth will have a child. In the prophecy that follows we are given in the words of the Hebrew Scriptures, a confirmation that John will be one of the ascetic Nazarites (Luke 1:15, Numbers 6:1-8). Having some doubt as to the possibility of that occurring, because as we are earlier informed, 'Elizabeth was barren, and both were advanced in years' (Luke 1:7) Zechariah, 'lacking faith and trust' is struck mute. We can only speculate as to the cause. There may well be some historical kernel here and if this was the case his being struck mute would appear to be something we would call psychosomatic. In a context of a very deep awareness of the sacred, likely in such an important sacred role he would carry out but once in his life, and/or profound guilt in the face of his lack of faith in the prophetic word given in such a sacred place, this is quite possible. Such psychosomatic cause may also be behind Saul/Paul's later being struck blind after a divine encounter and the subsequent guilt he was feeling, a guilt which was removed or resolved when Ananias lay hands upon him leading to his sight then being restored (Acts 9:1-19, 22:6-16). Within the Hebraic tradition Daniel had been struck dumb by such a divine epiphany (Daniel 10:15-17) while elsewhere we even read an account of how an encounter with the sacred can be so overwhelming to even cause a person to drop dead (1 Samuel 13:1-14)! Within the Christian Scriptures we find another episode of unresolved guilt concerning holy things causing the death (Acts 5:1-11). To return to our story we find Zechariah, struck dumb, being unable, at this once in a lifetime opportunity, to offer the priestly blessing which he ought (Numbers 6:24-26).

Again, in the telling of John's birth story we are in the realm of midrash, the parallel to this John the Baptist post-menopausal birth narrative being found as we have seen in a story central to the Jewish Scriptural tradition, that of Abraham and Sarah, who though both advanced in years, like Zechariah and Elizabeth, give birth to Isaac (Genesis 17, 21:1-7). The annunciation of a miraculous birth there is also accompanied, as here, by unbelief on Abraham's part (Genesis

17:17). Such barrenness, as earlier noted, for a woman was perceived as a great reproach in the tradition (Leviticus 20:20-21, Jeremiah 22:30) for in such a patriarchal society a woman's worth was largely measured by the children, especially male heirs, she produced. Further, every mother hoped to give birth to the Messiah and barrenness could only be understood as God's rejection of them as being worthy of being the vehicle of such (Genesis 30:23).

While John's birth is accompanied by some of the usual rituals such as circumcision (Luke 1:59), it is also marked by numerous events, 'which were talked about through all the hill country of Judea' (Luke 1:65). The most spectacular of the signs was Zechariah's ability to again speak upon his indicating that the child's name was to be John. Like many in the ancient world the Jewish people believed that a name was something much more than a mere nomenclature or label but rather signified something deep about the character and nature of the bearer. The name John was a shortened form of Jehohanan meaning 'God's gracious gift.' [2] Having thus named his son, Zechariah we are told, launches into a long prophetic exclamatory statement generally known as the Benedictus (this so called like the Magnificat and Nunc Dimittis, from the first word in Latin) (Luke 1: 67-80). The words therein contained pick up the same theme as the name John just given, namely that God is gracious. In style the Benedictus is like many found in the Hebrew Scriptures though it seems not to be a direct borrowing. The idea of 'the horn of salvation' draws on the vision of the ideal king overthrowing the nation's enemies (1 Samuel 2:10). In this context that must have referred to the hope that John would be the military leader to so overthrow the Romans. Finally, it is suggested that such wondrous things would come from John's birth it was hoped that it would cause, 'the bright dawn of salvation to rise upon us' (Luke 1:68) i.e. the beginning of the messianic age.

Luke by his very deliberate paralleling of the accounts of the events to do with the birth of the two figures makes it very clear that for him both John and Jesus belong together with John clearly subservient to the latter. This, as said, almost certainly does not reflect the historical reality. The forced way the parallel is drawn between the two probably

9: Who is the greatest?

indicates that, even at the time of writing, this certainly was not universally accepted as being the case. It is the old line 'thou doth protest too much' or if such is not reality then shout all the louder in attempting to compel belief. John was an important figure in his own right and almost certainly would not have understood himself as being only a precursor to Jesus. Josephus recognises his importance writes of him favourably as 'a good man [who] commanded the Jews to exercise virtue, both as to righteousness towards one another, and piety towards God' (Josephus: Antiquities of the Jewish People 18:116).

Following the narrative concerning his birth we are told that the Baptist spent his formative years in the desert. There has been much conjecture as to his relationship with the Essenes, perhaps even with the community at Qumran, the keepers, and almost certain authors, of the Dead Sea Scrolls. There are sufficient similarities in their views to give rise to this conjecture in both the Essene demand for bathing associated with ritual cleanliness and in the practice of asceticism, poverty and celibacy. That John was of priestly line also supports this premise as the Essenes, rejecting the temple establishment, understood themselves as forming a new purified priesthood serving in a new temple.

Let us turn now to examine the adult relationship between John and Jesus. John and Jesus certainly knew of each other and had met at least once, on the occasion of Jesus' baptism by John, yet as to his believing that Jesus was the Messiah, though it appears he acknowledges such on the occasion of this baptism, in reality it would seem John was uncertain as to Jesus' status even to his final days when, while imprisoned shortly before his execution, he sends some of his disciples to Jesus asking, 'are you the one who is to come, or do we look for another' (Luke 7:18-35)? Going again on the criteria of embarrassment whereby something is so well known that it can't be written out of the story despite the problems it causes, we can confidently hold that the account to do with John's final days and his doubting of Jesus is correct.

The connection and commonalities, on the other hand, between John and Jesus may be seen in both Herod and Jesus' disciples understanding of him as being John come back from the dead' (Luke 9: 7-9, 18-20, Mark 6:14, 8:28 and pars). By such belief the connection between the two, John and Jesus, in many minds, seems to be very tight. Further, there are connections in their message of justice and opposition to the established order, something which finds them both coming to a similar grisly end. The strongest connection lies in Jesus' baptism by John, an event present in four gospels, which as time goes on causes progressively more embarrassment (Mark 1:3-11 and through Matthew 3:13-17, Luke 3:21-22 and to John 1:29-34). Given the Christian understanding that Jesus was the one without sin why should he need a baptism carried out by John which had as its aim the remission of sin? Why should Jesus, whose pre-eminent status is clearly central to the Christian belief, seemingly place himself under John by such an action? Given the embarrassment factor again the evidence for the event is so strong it cannot be removed from the tradition and therefore must have occurred. The significance of the event then must over time therefore be increasingly tempered or explained in some way and this is what precisely happens in these accounts. Mark simply reports it, Matthew and Luke place words on the lips of John and Jesus to explain it, while John's gospel finds the act of such baptism so disturbing that it is excised but clearly underlies the narrative where Jesus encounters John while John is performing baptisms, but doesn't submit to such. With this baptism event we are, unlike in the infancy narratives of both figures, in the realm of history. Indeed, given that the testimony to this action is so great and causes such problems for all the gospel writers, it could be said that of all the stories concerning Jesus we are here on the most solid historical ground perhaps of any event associated with him.

It seems clear that Jesus was originally connected to John to the point of even submitting to his baptism. That causes severe embarrassment to the Christian movement who then must explain it away. By the end of John's life, he and Jesus are clearly differentiated hence John's questioning through his emissaries. Whether they at one stage worked together and had a falling out or merely a recognition that their views were at variance to each other we cannot know. There seems to be a clear divergence in religious practices between the disciples of Jesus and John with John and his disciples seen as ascetics while Jesus and his followers are seen to be 'gluttons and drunkards' (Luke 5:33-35,

9: Who is the greatest?

7:31-35). That difference probably comes about because of the different way they viewed God's kingdom. John understood it as something coming which would bring the world into judgment and one must best prepare oneself for that, while Jesus primarily understands God's reign as something largely already present. The symbol used by Jesus of the presence of the reign of God is the feast, particularly the wedding feast while John's is altogether harsher being associated with fiery judgment though that motif is not altogether absent from Jesus. This feasting image is central to Jesus' teaching and he also spent time at such celebrations (Matthew 25:1-8, John 2:1-11). Given his imaging of the reign of God as a marriage feast Jesus can make the retort to those criticising him and his disciples, 'can you make the wedding guests fast while the bridegroom is with them' (Luke 5:34)? This statement makes clear the distinction between the two. John understands himself as one who announces the coming judgment and reign of God understood as future, whereas Jesus understands that the presence of the reign of God is in some manner being already present, connected to his presence and being, for it is clearly he himself who is the bridegroom.

What did the two figures share? Of prime importance are the symbols used for their geographical location, their connection with the desert and the Jordan River. That association is important. Both the desert and the Jordan were reminders of the exodus from Egypt and subsequent military conquest of the Promised Land. Both the colonised Jewish people and the Roman colonisers and their collaborators would have equally known the significance of the location. For such overt political actions both John and Jesus were to share in execution at the hands of the political establishment they challenged. The cause for John's execution we are told in the Scriptures was for his criticism of Antipas' marriage to Herodias, this being judged by John as violating the Mosaic Law (Mark 6:17-29 and pars), but there is clearly more to it than that. Of John Josephus writes, 'others came in crowds about him, for they were greatly moved by hearing his words, Herod, who feared lest the great influence John had over the people might put it into his power and inclination to raise a rebellion, (for they seemed ready to do anything he should advise) thought it best, by putting him to death, to prevent any mischief he might cause' (Josephus: Antiquities of the Jewish People 18: 118). John's public opposition to Antipas' re-marriage may have served as the immediate reason for John's execution but it would have almost certainly been built on that wider critique which Josephus gives us. Of course, the whole gospel account of how Salome after dancing and being offered anything she wished, had John's head brought on a platter reads hardly factual. For a start who among the followers of either John or Jesus would have had access to Antipas' palace to know of such an event?

Jesus of course stands in that same rebellious line as John, suffering the same fate, execution, his by crucifixion, something reserved for sedition. That is confirmed most clearly by the discussion of 'kingdom' in his inquisition by Pilate (John 18:33-37) along with the words Pilate has placed upon Jesus' cross, 'the king of the Jews.' The level of Pilate's involvement in the execution of, 'just another rebel' is conjectural but whether the story reflects historical reality or not is not crucial. This, and the other Passion accounts, reflect the underlying belief by his followers concerning Jesus who acts seditiously by announcing a radical alternative kingdom to that which was official. He must therefore, in each of the gospel writer's accounts, come before Pilate the one who, in that geographical locale, was the symbol of Rome's rule. John's account, though highly stylised, makes the issues at stake very clear. Jesus is proclaiming an alternative kingdom to that of Rome and is therefore judged by Pilate as being seditious. It is hardly coincidental that Jesus acclaimed and charged with being 'king of the Jews' was put to death at the time of the great Jewish nationalist festival of Passover.

Though Luke has an agenda of trying to present the infant church as a respectable organisation he cannot hide the rebellious roots of the movement associated with both John and Jesus. The desert and Jordan had a connection, as said, understood by all, friend and foe alike, with the exodus of long ago. That journey had been a journey to freedom from the clutches of an imperial power, Egypt, to freedom, so in the context of another imperial power, Rome, now dominating Israel, the significance was clear. Knowing that, those powers, both imperial and

9: Who is the greatest?

subsidiary local, summarily deal with the challenge posed by John and Jesus as they best know how.

That John and Jesus represented distinctly independent movements can be seen in that the followers of John the Baptist are still present in the book of Acts (18:24-28, 19:1-7) and indeed to this very day in the Mandaeans found mainly on the border between Iran and Iraq, hardly a fortuitous place to live. If such a difficult geographical location were not enough they are not at all pleased with the Christians co-opting their great prophet and then making him subservient to their own!

In the Christian understanding, distinct as we have seen what was the probable historical reality, John the Baptist becomes the predecessor and forerunner of Jesus as the Messiah. Within Judaism it was widely expected that such a forerunner would come to announce the Messiah's coming. 'Behold I will send my messenger and he will prepare the way before me' (Malachi 3:1). This figure was identified with Elijah (Malachi 4:5) and it is with this figure that John the Baptist is identified in Christian understanding. There is a commonality about the desert locale, clothing and diet of Elijah and John to make this connection very clear (Matthew 3:4 c.f. 2 Kings 1:8). Of course, the Church was assisted in making such identification of John being the forerunner of the Messiah they identified as Jesus, by what no doubt was John's actual lifestyle and apparel.

What actual connection is there between John and Jesus? It would appear that in reality while there was an affinity about John and Jesus seen in their wilderness and Jordan location, in Jesus being baptised by John, commonalities in some of their themes, and in their common grisly end. There are however, distinct differences in how each, along with their disciples, lived and in how they imaged the reign of God and their role in it. While they initially seem to have been close, with Jesus even subservient to his older cousin, by the culmination of their ministries they were clearly treading distinct paths. Any attempt to fix them as part of the same movement with John being the subordinate one is clearly Christian propaganda not reflective of reality.

Luke has very deliberately paralleled the birth narratives of John and Jesus co-opting John from his own independent tradition and placing him in the Christian story making him clearly subservient to the main actor, Jesus. This reflects Luke's theological agenda as we have seen rather than the historical reality in which John the Baptist had established a messianic movement of his own, one which survived into the Christian era and indeed continues to this day. It is in their ministry however, linked to desert and Jordan and thus viewed as seditious, and the resultant executions at the hands of those they threatened, rather than in the birth narratives, so clearly framed by a theological agenda, that we find the true parallels between the two figures, John and Jesus. Another part of our Christmas story disappears, but again not without leaving us something important upon which to reflect.

Endnotes

1 The priesthood was divided into 24 divisions with that of Abijah being the eighth (1 Chronicles 24:10). Each division was assigned to duty for one week and lots were drawn each day to determine duties which could range from security, to being choristers, musicians and general servants right up to the privileged role which Zechariah was to carry out. As there were many thousands of priests and Levites they only had one opportunity to make this offering it not being permitted to perform it twice.

2 Names are significant right through this story. Thus, Zechariah signifies 'God remembers the covenant or agreement,' Elizabeth means 'God is faithful', John signifies 'God is gracious' while Jesus signifies 'God saves'.

10: Why the stories?

Having examined the stories, we may now turn to the question of the reason for their creation. Just why have Matthew and Luke created these infancy narratives, our Christmas stories? In asking this we need to remind ourselves once again that the earlier Christian writings of Paul and Mark know nothing of these infancy narratives while that the fourth gospel John, feels no need for an infancy narrative?

Clearly, we can surmise the early followers of Jesus were ever more deeply impressed with his significance both during and following his lifetime. It can only be conjecture of course but it would seem probable his initial followers viewed him as a wise teacher, then perhaps later a prophet before later again they seemingly began to understand him as the long-expected Messiah. Finally, almost certainly after his death, they came to see him in some sense as divine. Again, we need remind ourselves that this last claim regarding divinity is distinct from that of his being Messiah for the Jewish messianic hope nowhere included the idea that the Messiah had to be divine.

We need of course be cautious of the more elevated statements purportedly made both by and concerning Jesus in the gospels for they more reflect what the gospel writer has concluded concerning him some 40 years at least, even in the case of the earliest gospel Mark, after the events therein described, rather than any actual statements made by Jesus or others of him during the time of his ministry. In any case if Jesus himself had made them of himself they would be unattractive from his own lips, reflective more of a braggart with an elevated ego than one we would want to follow. As such I hold it was not Jesus but rather his disciples who began very early to ascribe these divine attributes to him. Once, however, the followers of Jesus concluded that in some sense he was divine they were then faced with the question, just when did he become so?

It should be noted that this ascription of divine status to Jesus happened very quickly, quite remarkable when we remind ourselves that this was all taking place within a strict Jewish monotheism. Some charge that the commencement of elevation to divinity upon Jesus, already present in the Christian Scriptures, comes from the Graeco-Roman world where such divine-human figures were common place. This represents an all too easy answer however for all the writers, with possible exception of Luke, ascribing this status to Jesus are from a Jewish background. [1] There clearly was something remarkable about this man which caused those from such a strict monotheistic background to come so quickly to view him as at least approaching divinity! Once having however made him divine a whole Pandora's box opened. How was Jesus divine, did he receive such divinity during his lifetime or was he divine from the very beginning? If he was divine how then did his divinity sit with his humanity for needs be he must be fully human as well as divine. The complexities of this seeming conundrum would exercise the Church for some 400 years until they were supposedly resolved in the Nicene Creed (late 4th century) and Chalcedon (5th century). That long wrestle with that question of the nature of Jesus' divinity began however, as I have said, much earlier, being present even in the Christian Scriptures themselves and the Christmas narratives are an important part of that.

For Paul, as we have already noted, divinity came to Jesus at his resurrection. He thus concludes, 'he was shown with great power to be the son of God by being raised from death' (Romans 1:4). There is, I know, a great deal of conjecture as to just what 'son of God' means but clearly Paul in a context of speaking about Jesus' resurrection means much more than that Jesus, like all of us is a son or daughter of God, or even that he is a significant figure or indeed Messiah, all these being caught up in this wide-ranging term, 'son of God.' For Paul the resurrection clearly cements an ontological status for Jesus as being uniquely 'son of God.' Paul is writing his epistles in the 50s and first half of the 60s of the 1st century CE with early date showing just how rapidly Jesus had been elevated to such a position! He even, as we have seen, uses what appears to be older material; hymnic or creedal statements which go back even further, perhaps to a time just after the life of Jesus, the best known being Philippians 2:5-11. In that passage, reaching back to the earliest layer of tradition, we find Jesus already having a distinct ontological status which he gives up in order to become human. Thus, of Christ we read, 'he was in the form of God, but did

10: Why the stories?

not count equality with God a thing to be grasped, but emptied himself, by taking the form of a servant, being born in the likeness of humanity' (Philippians 2:6-7). This is, as I have already claimed, a remarkable understanding of Jesus coming so early, and being transmitted through one, Paul raised in such a strictly monotheistic tradition, 'a Hebrew of the Hebrews'! (Philippians 3:5).

Contrary to Paul, Mark, writing some 10-15 years later, has Jesus receive distinct ontological status at his baptism where the heavens open and he is declared to be God's son in whom God is 'well pleased' (Mark 1:9-11). Again, there are arguments as to the meaning of 'God's son' but clearly the story is one making Jesus ontologically exceptional among others. Jesus is receiving now this elevated status, which clearly even in Mark's gospel is moving toward divinity, not at the resurrection as for Paul but rather at the commencement of his ministry.

This solution however is still not satisfactory for our infancy narrative writers, Matthew and Luke. They see a need to go a step further and place Jesus' distinct ontological status, at the point of his birth. To do this they, of course, develop birth narratives and as we have seen, do so by creating very different accounts. Lacking historical information on the birth of one so common as like Jesus they create, as we have seen again and again, events around Jesus' birth drawn from the sacred tradition using a method of midrash, while also making use of many of the common mythological motifs of the time. The motifs they use in these stories are clearly those designed to affirm this divine status of Jesus. By the time Matthew and Luke's writings I don't believe there is any question as to them ascribing some type of divine status to Jesus for I hold that to be precisely the goal of their nativity accounts.

The fourth gospel, John, still not satisfied with this solution as to Jesus' divinity, pushes back yet further that assumption of divinity. For John Jesus is co-existent with God from eternity as the divine Word through whom all things come with finally, this Word taking human form in Jesus (John 1:1-14). John either knows nothing of the birth narratives or chooses not to use them. If knowing them he probably judges them as being inadequate in dealing with the question of Jesus' assumption of divinity, instead preferring his own solution. His understanding of

Jesus' divinity being pre-existent from the beginning of creation is the view which prevailed, after that long spoken of almost half millennia debate as the orthodox understanding of the church.

The Christmas stories, increasingly loved however, survived, but not with the original purpose, ascribed to them by Matthew and Luke, indicating the point at which divinity was conferred upon Jesus. These stories, as judged by the Church, fail in their original purpose, superseded by John's understanding of Jesus' assumption of divinity, yet they not only survived but became central to the Christian experience. Clearly by the time of the triumph of the Johannine solution as to Jesus' ascription of divinity in the 4th and 5th century the popularity of the nativity of the nativity stories was sufficiently established though they had lost their original purpose. Indeed, it is from that time that we find, as we have seen, the first official celebrations of Christmas.

Yet in the modern era 'come of age' my contention has been that those things which through the ages attracted us about the Christmas stories are increasingly the things which today diminish their relevance for us. This diminution has come about because we can no longer believe in the magic around which these stories are built, with the consequence that we have then either rejected or sentimentalised them, the latter acting as a bulwark blocking our discovery of the powerful message not only present beneath the wrapping of the nativity stories. I believe there can be no greater dis-service to Jesus than to reduce his life to mere sentimentality. We fail in apprehending the depth of the Christmas narratives, and indeed faith as a whole, for we have a tendency, inculcated in us, to read them literally with little or no appreciation of the category of myth and the manner of truth which it conveys.

Once when we strip away the packaging; the magic, myths and legends, what are we left with of the Christmas story? I contend that we are left with the true miracle, which should be able to be more clearly seen for the lack of accretions, which if we are honest for us as modern human beings, get in the way either by presenting themselves as intellectually unbelievable, or by causing us to sentimentalize the story, or by a combination of both of those things.

10: Why the stories?

The kernel of the Christmas story is that it informs us that 'Emmanuel; God is with us.' God, rather than being the absent uncaring one, has chosen to be born in human form, open to all the vicissitudes which that human living brings. Gods taking human form however, as we have seen, were common in the ancient world. They did so however, as significant figures; the Alexanders, Caesars and other monarchs of the ancient world. The true miracle of Christmas is not then the divine entering the world in human form, a common enough thing, but rather the place in the gospel stories where God chooses to enter that form. Choosing not to enter in a place of prestige, power and might with worldly honour being due, the divine in Christ enters history on its underside, born scandalously of a peasant girl in a town, Nazareth, that represented nowhere, immediately becoming a victim of political oppression (at least according to Matthew), therefore being forced to flee as a refugee. Once we get past the literal question of whether these things happened or not, and as I have shown the majority did not, then we can get to the real issue; just what is the gospel writer saying about the divine presence in Jesus?

Christmas is primarily about the birth of a very different type of king into the world. This underside is still very much present in both the Matthean and Lukan stories even though they are intent on elevating this humble one to a place of honour. That elevation to honour is very deliberate, for such elevation and the methods employed to do so, enabled the contrast to be most starkly made between this one they understand as king, and other kings. Having been made a king this king's method of rule is shown to be very different, indeed in total contrast, to those with whom he is being compared. In order to achieve that elevation, the evangelists employ all the usual motifs associated with the coming of divinity into the world in antiquity. Thus, like other great heroes and kingly figures Jesus is given a special birth with all the wondrous events associated with it. In all the motifs used by both Matthew and Luke the claim is being decisively made that here is the one who comes as the true king/messiah, the one in whom divinity is truly present. This is of course a scandalous, even seditious action making this one, shamefully crucified by the empire, a king. Such action flies in the face of the Empire. Indeed, it even mocks the Empire along with all its claims.

Rulers in the ancient world were often styled as messianic figures of whom it was also promised would bring peace. Thus, we find placed on the temples of Asia dedicated to the Roman empire, specifically to Augustus Caesar, the words, 'providence...has in her beneficence granted us and those who will come after us (a saviour) who has made war to cease...with the result that the birthday of our God signalled the Good News for the world because of him therefore...the Greeks in Asia decreed that the New Year begin for all cities on September 23.' [2] We can begin to see in those words of peace echoed the words of the angels to the shepherds, 'good news' 'birth' 'saviour' 'peace' (c.f. Luke 2:11-14). Indeed, of both Octavius (to become Augustus) and Jesus it is said that they have come to bring a reign of peace so profound it even has cosmic effects. Of the former Virgil writes when describing the peace, he brings, 'even the merchant will give up the sea, the pine will not become a trading ship, for every land will furnish everything. The soil will not endure the hoe, nor vines the pruning hook.' [3] No work is even needed in Augustus' reign for Providence, identified with Augustus of course, is pleased to provide all. That same image likewise, but linked to Jesus, frames the last two chapters of the final book in the Christian Scriptures, Revelation (chapters 21-22).

Yet the parallel imagery is not only with the powerful figures of the pagan world but is also drawn with the great figures in Judaism. There is a very deliberate parallel drawn through midrash in these stories with such heroic figures in Judaism as Moses, Joshua and David. These were powerful figures in the classic sense of being so; strong, violent and often ruthless. Joshua and David carry out horrific acts of violence with their power being understood largely to come from those actions, in which it was claimed God was with them. Jesus is paralleled to them but that parallel is again used to very deliberately draw a sharp contrast with them. He, like them, is presented with the opportunity of power taken in the usual way yet, unlike them, refuses it. The Johannine line, 'my kingdom is not of this world' (John 18:36) is reflective of this. It is not that Jesus' kingdom has no effect in this world, being instead other-worldly

10: Why the stories?

as is usually understood by these words, but something far more deeply challenging. What is being said is that Jesus' kingdom cuts into the world in a most radical manner precisely in that it is not established by the ways and methods of this world. The reign of which Jesus speaks is worldly but not shaped by worldliness. In the synoptics Jesus is tempted with power in the usual way, right from the beginning of his ministry from where he is tempted in the desert, to its very end where the temptation comes in the guise of magically, thereby exhibiting great powers, coming down off the cross. Jesus refusal of such means of power is consistent. Jesus' kingdom is most certainly of this world precisely in that it is not worldly, not one exercised by worldliness and as such cuts most deeply into the world by precisely not being shaped by the world.

In co-opting the motifs associated with great rulers, both pagan and Jewish, the gospel writers are using them with deliberate subversive intent. As we have seen all those terms we so readily use of Jesus have their origin not with him but rather with the great rulers of the ancient world. When Jesus himself speaks of the kingdom or empire of God, and such speech and actions to do with this lie at the heart of his ministry, he is conducting a seditious act. Later when others speak of him in such terms as 'king,' 'messiah,' 'saviour,' and son of God,' they too join the conspiracy. In the Roman world there could be but one absolute ruler and one empire only, while to say otherwise was to act seditiously and thus essentially to seal one's destiny, almost always in such cases, execution. What the early Christian community, beginning from Jesus himself, did then was to appropriate these motifs of ruler and empire and apply them in a scandalous and clearly subversive manner both to their movement and to the one around whom it had been founded. The Romans clearly knew this and acted in accord with how they acted toward all seditious movements, first to Jesus, and later to many of his followers. It is this revolutionary critique of the power of Rome and the countering of its claims by positing another king/saviour/son of God, which frames our Christmas stories.

The Christmas stories proclaim then that a Messiah/king has come into the world but a very different style of king to the norm. We are thus challenged as to what type of rule do we pledge our allegiance. The motifs, symbols and myths of those other kingdoms and that inaugurated by Jesus may be similar, but they allude to very different types. The intentional use of the common myths as well as paralleling in midrash with messianic figures from the Hebrew Scriptures is designed to make this contrast all the clearer. It could almost be said that the gospels are making a 'spoof' of the claims to divinity and greatness by those of power, who are either making those claims of themselves or having them made of them. In that, Rome and its Caesars were particularly in mind but also their collaborators. The power of such people is to be understood to be completely subservient to this one in whom true power lies. Herod and his ilk have no place in setting Jesus' agenda, "Go tell that fox Herod, Behold I cast out demons and perform cures today and tomorrow and the day following; for it cannot be that a prophet should perish away from Jerusalem'" (Luke 13:32-33). The almost completely theological constructed story of Jesus before Pilate in John's gospel makes this abundantly clear. While it is Jesus on trial for his very life the gospel paints a clear picture reversing the mundane reality. It is Pilate, the empire he represents, and indeed the whole political project so often, then as now, made divine, which is on trial with Jesus standing as judge (John 18: 28-37).

As the biblical scholar Dominic Crossan states, 'twice within a hundred years, on different shores of that cruel and beautiful Mediterranean Sea, a man was proclaimed son of God when alive, and more simply God when dead.' One was Octavius, later called the august one, Augustus, the other Jesus, later called Christ. [4]

Why do we keep celebrating Christmas then? It may surprise many who started off reading this work believing it had as its goal the rejection of the Christmas story and its celebration, that I actually hope we still will continue to celebrate this festival. Indeed, such celebration in a fuller, deeper sense has been the aim of this work. Freed from the encumbrances which preclude us from authentically celebrating because, 'we can't believe,' or which cause us to sentimentalize it, thereby stripping it of its real power, my belief is that having examined the stories and uncovered the myths which frame them, we are freed to celebrate the true radical nature of what the narrative is actually about.

10: Why the stories?

I believe that in the Christmas story there is a deep truth spoken which moves far beyond the mere literalism of the event. The story tells us that there was something so remarkable about Jesus that it progressively led his contemporaries into an ever-deepening appreciation of him. They saw the way he lived as opening their lives to ever deeper dimensions. In him they experienced transcendence entering the mundane, eternity entering time and even the divine into the human. From being a teacher and charismatic teacher and healer, over time some understood him to be the long-awaited Messiah with some finally even daring to see him as divine; God enfleshed. From that perspective Christmas proclaims to us that God does not remain the absent God, but rather is found immersed in the midst of human history, specifically on its underside, to the point of fragile vulnerability. Given the totality of this immersion there can be no longer any 'God-forsaken place,' That is the remarkable nature of the Christmas stories. They, using and co-opting all the 'power' motifs drawn both from the scared tradition and the wider mythological sources, have the divine made present in the most vulnerable place, vulnerable initially as in the Christmas stories as a babe in the peasant world (think just what the infant mortality rate would have been for such a birth), and later vulnerable in the place in which the divine in Jesus opts to dwell, with the poor, oppressed and marginalised, with that then leading to the utter vulnerability of the cross upon which is brutally killed the one in which the fullness of Divinity has chosen to dwell.

The nativity stories are shaped both by the writers' experience of the adult Jesus and what that meant for them and by how they, the evangelists Matthew and Luke, creatively construct them using midrash, myth, magic and legend. In the light of such the Jesus of the infancy stories is presented as one of power, one to whom even the cosmic powers of space give praise. This power however is radically different to how such is exercised in the world both then and now. That radically different understanding of power shaped how Jesus carried out his ministry with then projected on to the constructed nativity stories.

In Jesus a new creation, as we have seen, has been inaugurated and the call now goes out for subjects to pledge their allegiance to this radically different style of rule.

The stories, using profound symbols tell us such things that in Jesus the transforming divine light has shone into the darkness, hence the brilliant star in Matthew's gospel and the glory of Luke's angel chorus. This one is so special that even his birth must be made different, hence it needing to take place in Bethlehem, the most propitious of all places, rather than in the back-blocks of Nazareth. Likewise, the special nature of the virgin birth, which is to be expected in the ancient world where divine-human liaisons were common, but which takes place in this instance not among the powerful, as was usually the case in antiquity, but with a peasant girl from the lowest of classes. As such the real miracle of the virgin birth resides in the one God chooses rather than ipso facto the virgin nature of the birth itself. This birth as such is then one that scandalises the respectable and proper who can only cast vindictive aspersions about it. Of course, this special one will announce a kingdom which stands at radical odds to the kingdoms of this world so that King Herod, as representative of those kingdoms of darkness, will of necessity using the most tyrannical method, seek to do away with the one announcing it.

We are not to pretend that the stories are history but rather to enter the experience and be transformed by them. As did the early Christians construct the narratives clothing them in their own symbols, myths and images, we need to engage with what the stories are affirming, perhaps in terms of new myths, images and symbols which have meaning to us. Then we will find the true meaning of Christmas. 'Emmanuel; God with us,' and in knowing that be transformed in our living by that belief, that belief then framing our actions in order to transform our world so that that exclamatory cry cried by Mary so long ago in the Magnificat may become reality rather than just hope.

Endnotes

1 This rapid rise is examined in Larry W. Hurtado, How on earth did Jesus become God? Eerdmanns, Michigan, 2005

2 Decree of calendrical change on a marble stela in an Asian temple dedicated to the Roman Empire and Augustus, its first emperor. Quoted in John Dominic Crossan: Jesus a Revolutionary Biography, Harper Collins, San Francisco, 1995: 1

3 Ibid: 3

4 Ibid: 2

www.ingramcontent.com/pod-product-compliance
Lightning Source LLC
Chambersburg PA
CBHW072153160426
43197CB00012B/2363